You too can do
the Texas Tango

Donna

Books by Donna Bocks

Lavender Blues
Came to Say Good-bye
Heartbeat of Home
Purple Prairie Schooner
Texas Tango
Twin Trees

TEXAS TANGO

Donna Bocks

Texas Tango
By Donna Bocks

Published by Open Window Creations

Donna Bocks, P. O Box 8231, Holland, Michigan 49422-8231.
DonnaBocks@birthAbook.com

ISBN: Texas Tango: 978-0-9802090-6-8
Project Development: *Open Window Creations*
Cover and Book Design: *Greystroke Creative*
Printed in the United States of America

Copies may be ordered from:

www.Lulu.com
DonnaBocks@birthAbook.com

Acknowledgments

How does a 78 year-old get the desire and courage to finally bring her six typewriter-written novels out of the basement, and into the hands of a reader? By reaching out for lots of support!

In the beginning, I was a writer of stories, and received encouragement, feedback, and knowledge from Donna Winters, Dennis Hensley, the Writers Digest School, the Midwest Writers Workshop, and the Herrick District Library Writers Group. Thank you!

In June 2009, I attended a workshop facilitated by Patricia Lynn Reilly, Publishing Coach and so much more. She challenged me to bring my six novels out of the basement and into the hands of a team that produced the book you're holding in your hands! Many thanks to her team of editors, designers, and assistants.

Throughout the years, I've been mother, grandmother, and friend, and my family and friends have supported me, unconditionally. A special thanks to my children and their spouses who joined Patricia's team to illustrate, digitize, and read the typewritten manuscripts on their way into your hands.

Each word in the novel you're reading, expresses my thanks…

For Rita who opened the world of horses to me...

 CHAPTER 1

It was early afternoon and the wind had turned blustery. James stepped into a doorway to catch his breath.

A figure was fighting to get across the square, head down, butting the wind.

James spotted an old rusted pick-up truck lurching down the street. There were college boys racing along next to the vehicle, some standing on the running board. They were whooping it up like Mack Bennett's Keystone Cops.

They seemed to be having a wild time. Maybe they were practicing to enter the homecoming parade, James mused.

He was on the verge of laughing at the commotion. Instead, the sound lodged in his throat.

A gust of wind had caught the walker crossing the square as the person stepped from the curb and fell. The person could not seem to get back up.

The truck sped up, heading for the downed walker. The boys were making hideous noises. The woman was cringing in the gutter. James took off running at full speed.

The truck swerved, careening around the corner with screeching tires; then the rowdy boys were gone.

James reached down to help the person onto the grassy area between the road and the sidewalk.

"It's my ankle." As the person spoke, the hood of her jacket fell onto her slim shoulders. James was taken aback. It was a young woman. A very beautiful young woman. She was trembling. Each of them was gulping— she from the near-death experience and he from the running. They sat trying to slow their heartbeats. James tried to consider how he now found himself in this situation.

At twenty-nine, James felt he'd made a mistake by returning for the fall term at the University of Texas/Odessa. The weekends were too long. Football games, parties, and foolishness just didn't cut it this time around. He wanted to get in, get out, and move on with his life.

It was because of his restlessness that he had hopped into his old green Ford. Parking near the campus area, he walked around just to stretch his legs. This experience with the rowdy kids and the beautiful young woman reverberated like an explosion in his sluggish existence.

Recovering his voice, he said, "My car is close by. If you can stand, I'll drive over and pick you up. Grab hold of the pole for the street sign to steady yourself. I'll see that this is reported to the police, but first let's attend to you."

She hesitated, trying to put pressure on her foot. The pain was excruciating.

To assure her he said, "I think you should have it checked in Emergency. Would you prefer that I call someone you know? I'd wait with you 'til they arrived."

James watched her as she studied his face, wondering if she should trust him.

"I would appreciate a ride. You could drop me off, then I'll make further arrangements." She appeared worried.

He headed for the car, thinking he should hurry before her foot began to swell. Pulling up, he helped her into the back seat so she could elevate her leg.

The hospital was only a few blocks away. He drove slowly so as not to jolt the foot, and to keep her calm. The drive took five minutes.

James helped her inside. She wrote her name on the list at the nurses' station. After guiding her to a seat, he left to pull the car into a parking space.

When he reappeared she was surprised. "You shouldn't have to sit here by yourself," he explained. "Let me help you with your coat." He went to the rack in the corner of the waiting room and hung both of their jackets on the same hook.

He could feel her watching him. She was probably wondering if she was safe in his presence

"Cindy Fillmore?"

As she attempted to stand, the nurse said, "Let me get a wheelchair. Would you like your friend to come in with you?"

Cindy smiled weakly and said, "Come on, Walter, I'm not feeling too great." James jumped to his feet and followed her into the curtained corner.

"The doctor will be with you soon. Lie back and keep the foot up. I'll bring you an ice pack."

"Why Walter?" asked James as he leaned forward in the chair.

"Sir Walter Raleigh. You know, the puddle and cape story. You'll have to pretend about the puddle and cape, but you must admit you were gallant."

Laughing heartily he said, "I remember that one. But my name is James Pride. I'm from Texas. Now don't laugh. The way the saying goes: 'There's Texans and those that wish they was.'"

"At least you know who I was referring to, and that's refreshing. I've been teaching history for three years. I decided to come to the campus and get my master's. Got my B.A. in Michigan. Decided a different school and new surrounding would perk things up a bit. It sure did."

"I'm, sort of, in the same situation. I've been working for five years and have decided the extra classes I needed would go faster if I stayed at school and concentrated on my studies. I'm picking up some graduate business courses. I figure I'll need the background to have the ranch continue to be profitable in the future."

A doctor came in and examined her carefully. A volunteer wheeled Cindy down to X-ray. James tried to concentrate on the magazine he was paging through, but all he could see was the girl's face . . . expressive eyes, they almost matched her light auburn hair. Not a blemish. She was a masterpiece.

When they returned and the nurse helped her back up on the bed, Cindy grimaced and turned white. She lay with her eyes closed for a moment. James stared at her, still finding no imperfections.

She opened her eyes slowly and smiled. "Do you often read Teen magazine?" He could feel his face coloring.

"You remind me of the bricks on the outside of my apartment building." Her hesitation toward James was evaporating. Just before closing her eyes again she reached for his hand.

The doctor hurried in. "Nothing broken." He flipped through several papers on a clipboard. "Get her home and see that she rests. I'm giving her a few samples of a pain medication. She's to soak that foot and periodically use an ice pack. They're bringing crutches from the pharmacy."

One of the nurses pulled the curtain aside and asked the doctor to come out to the reception desk. James would be glad to get out of the hospital. He always felt jittery around these efficient women in white. There was a certain swish to their uniforms as they went about their duties that set him on edge.

The doctor was back in minutes. "Let's see, where was I? The pharmacy will also bring an elastic ankle brace that she is to use when the swelling is under control. Don't let her throw that away; she may find it handy from time to time."

"Her sleepiness is due to shock to her system. Sometimes a jarring like that will produce those results. She's fine. Cindy, are you listening?"

Her eyes opened slowly in response.

"Follow my instructions. You'll be laid up a day or so, and it will slow you down a bit for a few days. Get an appointment with your doctor after a week or so, just so she can check things out."

He looked at James. "It's a good thing you were with her." With those words he was gone.

• • •

Back in the car again James asked, "Well, young lady, where do you live?"

"It's a short distance. Turn left from the parking lot. Down three blocks, on the corner. It's a large . . ."

"Brick building. I know."

"As long as you've gone this far, will you see that I get up the stairs? I don't know how I can ever thank you."

"No problem."

He pulled up in front of the building. Opening the car door, he scooped her up in his arms and wrestled with the crutches. Awkwardly, they made it to the second floor.

James bent his head to look into that pretty face. She reached for his wide-brimmed hat saying, "I'll carry this." At the same time, Cindy rummaged for the key in her jacket pocket.

Her apartment was a small bed-sitter with a tiny cooking alcove. Snug, but homey.

James deposited her in the corner of the sofa bed and went to the fridge to see if there were ice cubes.

He overheard her dial the phone and ask for Brad. "I have to cancel on the dance and party tonight, I fell and . . . Later then."

Finding a plastic tub under the sink, he filled it with ice cubes and cold water.

"Is the bathroom down the hall?"

"Do you need it? Or do you think I need help getting there?" She tried to smile, but her ankle was throbbing.

"I was concerned about you."

"I used the one at the hospital. I'm fine for now."

He felt an urgency to be on his way. Her friend might be on his way. Scribbling his phone number on a piece of paper he said, "In case you need anything."

• • •

Sunday seemed to last forever. James lost count of the number of times he'd had his hat and jacket on. Most likely her friend was looking after her. He'd sure have been watching over her if she was his girl.

A week passed before he spotted her on campus. His attention span in classes had been on a low level and his studies were suffering, and so was he. He nodded his head, and she waved.

His desire was to approach her, but she was walking with several classmates.

The rest of the week he waited nearby so he could catch a glimpse of her. Her hair fascinated him. It was so shiny, and each time he saw her it was fixed in a different way. It was twisted and rolled and braided, and sometimes a combination of more than one thing. It added to her already lovely face. He wondered what her hair would look like loose and soft, lying on her shoulders.

Another miserable weekend passed.

As Cindy and the girls from the apartment building walked to class the next week, one of them asked, "Who was the cowboy who had eyes for you last week?"

"He's the one who helped me when I fell. Guess he just wanted to make sure I survived. I imagine he has a girl back home."

• • •

"James! Phone's fer you."

He hurried down the stairs. "Hello, Dad. Is anything wrong?"

"I'm sorry," claimed the female voice.

"Who is this?"

"Cindy Fillmore. Should I call another time?"

James stood looking at the fellas, all standing and grinning in the kitchen doorway.

"Hello. Do I have the right number?"

"Beat it, you guys." In explanation he said, "I live in a rooming house, Cindy, and private phone calls are hard to come by."

"We can fix that. How about coming for supper tomorrow night. I owe you for helping me out. Say 6:00?"

"Sounds great." The others had lost interest and were watching TV.

James put on his hat and went for a walk. He couldn't stop smiling. At least he'd get to see her again.

 CHAPTER 2

At 6:00 the following evening he knocked on her door.

"Come on in."

Cindy had her back to him. Her hair was cascading down her shoulders. She hadn't seemed like the domestic type, so he was surprised to see that she had an apron on. James glanced at the table. It was set for only two. He had been worried that the meal might include her friend Brad; that it would be a polite "thank you" and a very uncomfortable hour or so.

"Will you stir this while I put everything else on the table?"

She turned around. James was still standing by the door. Her eyes said, I trust you. The pale pink lipstick enhanced her faint smile. He moved toward her and managed to stumble over his own feet.

"That first step is a killer," she warned humorously, and her smile spread full and welcoming.

"I didn't make anything fancy, but it should taste good."

Minutes later James declared, "It's terrific." That was the truth. Some lucky guy would win the heart of this multitalented beauty. He wondered if he was being foolish even to throw his hat in the ring of competitors.

They remained fairly quiet as they leisurely enjoyed the meal. It was a comfortable quiet.

Cindy brought him warm apple pie and coffee. No more stumbling; he had to know some things.

"So, the healing process moved right along?"

"Not really. That Sunday was terrible. I'm ashamed to admit, I fell apart. It hurt worse and I can't afford to miss classes. But, I finally got everything caught up. It was hard to get around."

"Didn't your friend . . . help out? The one you contacted?"

"Brad? The minute he found out I was in pain and couldn't party he lost interest. Haven't heard from him since."

"I wish you had called." James was afraid to utter another word for fear of giving his feelings away.

"If I wash the dishes will you dry? I have to keep everything up to snuff in a place this small."

They worked side by side until the task was completed.

As Cindy turned to hang up her apron she asked, "Are you always so helpful to strangers?"

"I am because I hope they will become my friends."

He slipped his jacket on in preparation of leaving.

"James, may I ask you a personal question before you leave?" She did not wait for his reply, but continued, "Is there a woman waiting for you back home?"

He shook his head no, unable to speak.

She placed her hand in his. "Then do you suppose we could be friends? I have your phone number. Would you care to have mine?"

He had walked halfway home before he remembered that he had driven his car. Sheepishly, he hurried back the three blocks. He was going to hop in the car and make a quiet getaway.

Lights blinking off and on above him drew his attention. Cindy was standing in the window, laughing, and holding his hat. He wasn't embarrassed; he didn't care. She raised the window and in a loud whisper said, "Pick it up tomorrow night."

As James drove away there were tears in his eyes. In his twenty-nine years there had been girls, and women. He liked them, and one or two had interested him, but not as much as the ranch.

They would have been willing partners, but somehow they could not hold his attention. There was always an emptiness in the relationship. The void was as endless as the creek beds that ran throughout Jeff Davis County.

Mom,

It was so good to hear your voice on my birthday. The card, with check enclosed, arrived in the next day's mail. I can sure use it. Thanks.

I am managing well with expenses, but every little bit helps.

In my last letter I mentioned that I fell, twisting my ankle pretty bad. I didn't call because I didn't want to worry you, etc., etc. It's just fine now.

The story has another "twist" to it. I was trying to get back on my feet when I heard footsteps. A young man, from Texas, drove me to the hospital, and saw that I got home safely.

I invited him to supper this evening, to repay his kindness. Have I mentioned that he's just a little taller than me and extremely good looking, in a rugged sort of way?

I will say this—I hope he's interested in me because it would be easy for me to be interested in him.

25 and still ticking.

I'll write.

Cin

P.S. I know you'd like him.

James called her about 4:30 to see if she'd like to go out and get a burger. When he arrived at 6:00 she had her jacket on. As James took the hat from her he shook his head, and looked puzzled. "I have never left that hat anywhere. It's part of me."

Although Cindy said nothing, she seemed to hesitate for an instant before releasing it.

They stepped into the hallway. "So, actually you left a bit of yourself with me. Thank you." And she turned to lock the door. "Let's walk. It's quite nice out."

There was litter along the sidewalk. It wasn't far to The Big Burger. It was crowded and noisy inside. As soon as they had eaten James said, "Let's get out of here." The door closed on the noise.

They strolled down by the pond. It was beginning to get dark and the ducks had nestled their beaks among their feathers. James and Cindy sat close on a bench as the evening chill began to penetrate their jackets.

James turned and asked, "Could we spend some time together this weekend?"

"I have to study on Saturday. I don't dare ask you over to study because I wouldn't be able to keep my mind on the classwork." He squeezed her hand. "Me either. How about Sunday? Say I was to come by at 10:00 and we could make a day of it?" She nodded. "That would be swell."

With that they headed home.

"I'm going to leave you here at the outside door. If I take you to your door I fear that I might leave my hat again." With that he turned and walked to his car.

• • •

Sunday it was warm and the skies were clear. When James pulled up in front, Cindy was waiting on the steps. He pushed the door on the passenger side open and she hopped in.

As they drove down the highway James said, "There's a small town not far from here with some shops, and there's a little restaurant there that's got a nice menu. Does that sound okay?"

Cindy nodded her head in agreement. They both relaxed and took in the scenery.

They pulled into the town parking lot around 11:00. The shops were starting to open their doors. It was nice enough to prop them open, which encouraged browsers to wander in and out.

The crowds hadn't worked up an appetite yet, so the Village Bistro was empty except for a couple at one of the tables in the back. James and Cindy seated themselves in a quiet corner.

The menu was written on an old chalkboard.

Everything   **Made from**
fresh   **scratch**

Sunday
A cup of onion soup
Warm homemade rolls with unsalted butter
Small salad greens topped with cheese grated at your table
Charcoal grilled pork loin chop
Fresh vegetables   Small red potatoes
Hazelnut coffee   Crème brulee

No choices   **Be prepared to relax**

Cindy put her hand to her mouth. "Gracious sakes, it's a good thing I just had toast and juice for breakfast."

James smiled. "I thought it would give us time to talk."

And so it did. The afternoon drifted slowly by. If the bistro served its clientele, James and Cindy never noticed. Their world encompassed a table, two chairs, delicious food, revealing conversation, and the soft glow of a candle.

They rode home in complete silence, each within his and her own thoughts.

James was thinking about the girl sitting next to him in stirrup pants and a very stylish sweater, in his favorite pale blue color that did nothing to camouflage her figure. Her delicate hands rested in her lap.

Although Cindy appeared to be daydreaming, her mind was focused on the man in the driver's seat. Dark hair and eyes and a determined chin. She almost reached over and stroked his smooth cheek. Then she swallowed hard attempting to move her thoughts to safer ground.

James parked the car and got out to open her door. He followed her up the stairs. Cindy unlocked the door, but before opening it she said, "Entering this apartment could be dangerous."

"I hope so."

She placed their jackets on the back of a folding chair and laid his hat on the card table.

As she turned back toward him, he folded her into his arms and kissed her. Finally, she tapped him on the shoulder. He looked at her, questioning the gesture.

"I think my shoes have melted and I'm stuck to the floor."

With that he swept her off her feet and sat on the sofa with her in his lap.

They held each other tightly for a long time.

"I can't stay or the situation will become more than dangerous."

"I know."

She stood. He kissed her on the nose, and picked up his hat and jacket as he headed out the door. James turned and said, "I'll call."

Cindy hung up her jacket and readied for bed. She thumbed through a couple of magazines, and she had just turned the light out when the phone rang.

"Hello."

"It's me. I'm not at the rooming house. I'm calling from the pay phone outside of the drug store. I had such a fine day."

"I think that should be my line."

"I guess I just wanted to say good night."

"Good night, James." She placed the phone gently back into its cradle.

James wondered if he should feel foolish. Getting to sleep would not be easy. He was hopelessly in love. Maybe admitting it to himself would clear a path in his mind.

The balance of October was whisked away. November was filled with classes and studies and long walks.

Cindy purchased a bright-flowered cloth to cover the card table. Usually both folding chairs were filled, for light meals and heavy discussions. The little bed-sitter was like a protective nest from the outside world.

Cindy was reading the newspaper one evening and began to laugh. "Here's just what you need, James. For Sale, Rottweiler: 5 months old, trained to answer commands of sit and down. Also shakes hands, and is a good dancer."

"That reminds me, I found just the thing for your Christmas gift. It's a big green frog. You set it outside your door and every time someone walks by it makes a croaking sound. Certainly a practical item, and every home should have one."

"In that case, I won't have to waste a lot of my valuable time shopping for you, will I?"

"With those kind words I'm going to depart for home. The guys have been ribbing me about not spending much time there. I tell them as long as I show up nights. . . ." With that he raised both hands and tried to look neglected. "You done with that paper? I need something to put my shoes on, they need a good shine."

One Saturday night, they were sitting on the floor leaning against the sofa with a big bowl of popcorn between them. Cindy moved the bowl and slid over next to James; that placed their feet side by side. "Look at those big feet."

"The better to hold me up with, my dear."

"Look at those strong hands and arms and shoulders."

"The better to catch you with, my dear." Cindy started to move away but James pinned her. "If you are going to move away from me, then give me back the popcorn."

"I'm caught in a trap, and I can't fetch the bowl, kind sir."

"Too bad."

• • •

The week before Thanksgiving, James asked if Cindy would try to make it back home over the short vacation. She indicated she'd be going home over Christmas instead.

Overjoyed, he clasped both of her hands in his. "Will you do me the honor of coming to the ranch? I really want to show you the place. You'll love my dad. You can meet Aunt Mildred and Fred and my grandpa. Aunt Millie's a marvelous cook. And . . ."

She put her hands to his lips and smiled. "The honor would be mine."

James knew he was bubbling like a child who wanted to tell about his first trip to the rodeo.

"Can I use this phone?"

"Of course."

It was only seconds before the phone was answered.

"Dad, it's James. . . . I know, I've just been so busy. I'm bringing home a friend over the holiday. Yes, I want to talk to her, too. No, Aunt Millie, that won't do. She'll need a separate room." He knew his face must be the color of his aunt's raspberry jam. "We'll pull in late Wednesday afternoon."

After he hung up he explained, "My aunt has changed some things around and my room has twin beds now."

Was this the same young man Cindy had met in September? He had seemed like such a take-charge person. At the moment he seemed filled with childhood joy, almost as though he was going to dance around the room.

• • •

Mom,

I haven't written as often as I planned. James and I have been busy. It's a nice name, isn't it? I am so very fond of him. That's a foolish statement. I'm almost afraid to express my true feelings for fear that it is a dream.

You knew that I wasn't planning on coming home 'til the Christmas holiday. Well, I have been invited to the ranch. It's a guest ranch and James wants to give me the grand tour.

Love you,

Cin

Happy Thanksgiving!

Cindy saw very little of James during the following days. They had decided that they would leave Wednesday noon as soon as classes were excused.

James had never been late before. It was after 1:00 when he showed up. He came racing up the stairs. She opened the door to an excited young man with a flushed face.

"Come on, quick, before there's more trouble." Before she had time to ask any questions he had her rushing down the stairs.

"Hurry, before she gets away again. That's why I'm late. She was running all over the backyard and I had all the fellas out trying to catch her."

Cindy looked past James at the grinning Rottweiler pup looking out the car window. "And what might her name be?"

"Dancer. Come on, I'll tell you all about it."

 CHAPTER 3

James got Cindy settled in with Dancer on her lap before he climbed into his seat. After sitting still for a minute, he turned; putting his hand behind Cindy's head he leaned toward her to give her a kiss. Wanting to be part of the family, Dancer started generously joining in.

Cindy yelled, "Stop, both of you. Too much."

James had barely started the car when Cindy exclaimed, "I hate to complain, but Dancer is all excited and is leaking on me."

"Oh, boy! As soon as I get to the edge of town I'll put her choke chain and leash on and get her out for a little walk. I've got an old blanket in the trunk that you can put between her and your clothes."

It wasn't long before everything was straightened around and Dancer was asleep.

Once James had shared Dancer's story he stopped short. "You do like dogs, don't you? I thought she could be ours, only for now she'd be better off at the ranch."

"Do they know you're bringing her to stay?"

"It will be fine. I've got to admit I seem to be a bit unhinged lately. But that's all your fault."

"My fault!"

"Shh! Don't wake the pup." And he looked at her out of the corner of his eye.

The miles rolled by; and the pup slept soundly. Several times James reached over and lightly brushed Cindy's hand. As they neared the ranch he began telling the history of the area.

• • •

Anyone at the ranch would observe an interesting scene. In one of the barns, at the end of the drive, a man was trying to look genuinely busy, yet nonchalant. It had passed 4:00, and he was obviously listening for a certain car. He repeatedly moved to the barn door.

A woman casually stepped to the kitchen window, wiping her hands on a towel. Then she'd go to the stove and stir some homemade potato soup, then to the cooling rack to take a whiff of the apple pie one more time. The kitchen was full of good smells in preparation for tomorrow's dinner.

On the second floor, sitting in a rocker by the window, was an older gentleman of eighty-five. As the time dragged on he began to rock faster.

The woman setting the table realized that the rocking had ceased: she held her breath and listened.

The car whirled into the drive. Two car doors flew open. A small dark figure scampered wildly around the yard. The occupants of the car were frolicking with the dog and laughing.

The man strolled out of the barn with a smile from ear to ear.

The woman went rushing out through the screen door; directly behind her was a small gentleman moving as if a firecracker had exploded underneath his rocking chair.

A trio of voices sang out, "Jimmy!"

Cindy looked at James and let her smile glow. Raising her eyebrows she said, "Secrets?"

He placed his arm around her shoulder and presented her to his family. "This is my . . . best friend, Cindy Fillmore. My father, Samuel James Pride. My grandfather, S. J. Pride. My favorite and only Aunt Mildred. I am officially known as James Samuel Pride.

"Now to start over. Cindy, this is Sam, Gramps, and Aunt Millie. And in my home territory my handle is Jimmy."

Then there was another face in the crowd. He was identified as Fred, Aunt Millie's husband, a man who said little.

Gramps spoke up. "Who is this little lady sitting in the middle of this happy circle?"

"That's Dancer."

Gramps continued, "Bet a pair of long Johns that you been lettin' her sleep with you. Take her out to the barn. You know where she goes."

The welcomes, hugs, and glad-to-be-here's were passed around.

Jimmy took Cindy's hand and coaxed the dog toward the barn. Aunt Millie hurried in to finish supper. Sam and Gramps followed to pester her while she worked and to talk her out of a cup of coffee.

"Why didn't you tell me you were called Jimmy?"

"It sounds out of place at the university. Come here, Dancer." He picked her up and put her inside a boxed area with straw on the floor. She began to whimper. "I feel bad too, but the house rules are different here."

As they approached the barn door James drew Cindy to him and kissed her long and hard. "Have I told you how much I . . . care for you?"

"Let's see, in flowery words you introduced me as your best friend and in private you just told me that you care for me. Yet, when you kiss me you turn my legs to rubber bands and I almost collapse. I'm going to be blunt with you Jimmy Pride. I love you."

"Has anyone ever made love to you in a hay mow?"

With that, Cindy broke away from him and ran for the house, calling back, "I'll bet supper's waiting."

After supper things were cleared away Aunt Millie and Cindy did all they could toward final preparations for the following day. Then they sat down for a minute at the kitchen table to rest.

Cindy confessed, "When I left school I made sure I was presentable to meet you all. As Jimmy told you, the dog was a surprise to me. In her excitement she wet on me a little, then slept on my lap the balance of the trip. I was afraid you might get an odd impression of me."

Aunt Millie reached for her hand. "My dear, you don't need to worry about the impression you've made on this family. We can't love you as Jimmy does, but we are in line right behind him. Don't be embarrassed, there's no way the two of you can hide that fact."

"I'll tell you a secret. After Jimmy returned to school this time, Gramps went downhill. Spent more and more time in his room. He lost interest in the ranch. It wasn't like him. We were really concerned. He's even been using a cane from time to time. The two of you have rekindled his spirit. I couldn't believe it when he appeared right behind me when you pulled up."

They went into the family room where the men were discussing what had taken place while Jimmy was away.

Aunt Millie announced, "I'm showing this young lady to her room, and I'm turning in. I've got to get up earlier than usual tomorrow to make stuffing and pop the turkey in the oven."

Cindy said, "See you men in the morning." They climbed the stairs and Aunt Millie opened the door to a pretty room done in light blues and white. "Be sure and wake me early so I can help."

Thanksgiving Day was brisk and cloudy, but no one noticed. They explained that they took no guests at the ranch over this weekend. It was the one time during the year that they spent alone as a family. It seemed appropriate. This enabled all the help to be with their families, too. The four men took care of any necessary chores.

The meal was always the same; turkey, dressing, mashed potatoes and gravy, squash, Jell-O salad, homemade bread and jam, and pumpkin pie with whipped cream. And, naturally, plenty of hot coffee. It was stressed that Gramps always had dibs on the gizzard, however. Age did have its privileges.

After everyone was seated Sam asked, "Fred, will you say a word?"

They bowed their heads. After a moment of silence, Fred spoke up, "I just think that the folks sittin' 'round this table have so darn much to be thankful for, and they don't know how to react to joy and happiness anymore."

Everyone smiled and said, "Amen."

The smiles grew and were passed around with the mashed potatoes and gravy. The sounds of celebration were something to remember. Each person looked at the other with a gift of love and appreciation. Everything tasted extra good.

Cindy and James went out to feed and play with Dancer.

A family. Cindy's heart almost ached with pleasure.

• • •

James had declared the day after Thanksgiving as tour-the-ranch day.

The night before, Cindy couldn't keep her eyes open. Everyone had turned in earlier and Cindy lay sorting out her thoughts about the past day and a half.

Thinking of James as Jimmy was easier than she might have thought. He had been right, she had felt love from, and for, his family immediately. All of a sudden she was startled with a realization.

There was lots of open, general, conversation floating around. Both Gramps and Aunt Millie had talked to her. Naturally, she and Jimmy had talked several times off by themselves.

But, Sam had addressed very few words directly to her. He was always at ease and smiling, and he appeared to be extremely satisfied with the situation. But he made no attempt to talk to her personally. Several times when she had looked up quickly, she had caught him studying her.

Recalling this, she felt bad. Maybe he was waiting for her to make the first move. Tomorrow she would have to try to correct that.

Cindy woke early. She dressed and went downstairs. Thinking she smelled coffee, she wandered into the kitchen. Sam was standing by the counter adding cream and sugar to his cup.

"You're up bright and early, Cindy. We may have to put you to work cleaning out stalls. I've been wanting to catch you by yourself. Grab a cup of coffee and join me in my office." She trailed shyly along behind him into a room she had not entered before.

For a minute Sam turned toward his desk. Cindy sipped her coffee and walked slowly around. The room had a very private look. Book shelves were awry, but what an eclectic range of interests. There was a smell of leather; an outdoor working man's study. The word virile came to mind.

Her coffee cup rattled as she stood facing him.

"Have a seat." All traces of a smile had vanished. His desk was huge and old and beautifully preserved. It was covered with papers and record books. Organized disorder?

He realized she was leaning forward squinting at a small picture he had just moved aside. "It's Gramps and Jimmy and me."

"I'm staring at the mustache."

"He shaved it off the morning he went back. Gramps and I are clean-shaven but most of the boys around here wear them."

"So, you love my son, do you?"

Her coffee cup repeated its movement in the saucer a second time. Timidly, she spoke up, "Yes, Sir." Then she sat up and looked at him equally. "Yes, Sir, I certainly do." The stillness seemed to grow thick and heavy, like a door to a bank safe after hours. Maybe this was a forbidden door. Was she unwelcome after all? She was afraid to breathe.

"Good." With that declaration she almost tumbled from her chair; the cup and saucer began to adhere to one another. Sam tried very hard to conceal his smile.

"He seems more settled than I've ever seen him. He's looked for you a long time. Never seemed interested in anyone before. Went out, and all that. I was afraid the ranch was going to be his mistress of the mountains. I'm sure she'll always be second. But it gives me a good feeling that the first place has been taken up by a lovely young woman like yourself."

"I think I hear Millie rattling around in the kitchen. Let's go and see what's for breakfast."

Additional faces appeared at the table. Sam explained that these were some of the unattached ranch hands. The large dining area wouldn't be open until Monday morning. "I might add this is the nucleus of the staff. This is LC, and Buc Wilson. Coming through the doorway is Tim Tyler and his son Randy. This is Cindy Fillmore, a guest of Jimmy's."

Just then Jimmy came whistling through the door. "Morning, everyone. Glad you're up Cindy. Eat hearty, because we've got a big day ahead of us. What's good for breakfast today, Aunt Millie?"

"Everything."

"Ah, just as I remembered. Love this place. Maybe you can teach Cindy how to make biscuits like yours." With that, the ranch hands each gave Cindy a serious look.

After the young couple had gone outside, Gramps joined the group at the table. Finally, one of the men spoke up. "A mighty pretty filly. I don't know about her bloodlines, but her lines are sure nice."

Sam left to do work in his office. Gramps kept his eyes on his plate. After a few more minutes of silence, the men left to do their work.

Jimmy was talking a mile a minute. This was a subject he was totally familiar with. "We can host about two hundred people here on the ranch if we use the bunkhouses. That's what we do when the school kids are here. Adults stay in nice cabins with private baths. There are all kinds of programs. Ecology is stressed in all of them."

"There are horses to ride. For some, it will be the first and possibly the last time that their lives will include that adventure. I was brought up on horses. Life would be a big letdown for me if it didn't include them. I hope we have time before we leave to go out and see Buffer: that's short for Buffalo. He's out to pasture while I'm at school."

Turning to face Cindy, Jimmy took hold of her forearms. He stood still, looking so serious, it made her uncomfortable. "Usually, I'm a rather somber person. Oh, I have fun; but there's a lot to do to keep life moving along on the right track. Do you understand what I'm saying?"

"You used the word unhinged on the way here. Am I having a bad influence on you? I'm not meaning to cause distress to anyone."

"Listen to me. I have always been happy; as a child and as a man. But you have brought a glow into my life that has never been there before. It's like you have opened a window and a fresh breeze is blowing in. My heart is bursting with exuberance. I have never felt more alive. Now the future holds promise; it's not just filled with what I like to do and will continue to do, it's also overflowing with new ideas."

"This land has a wonderful past. Now I am beginning to see its future more clearly. It's a lot of hard work and long hours. This weekend I'm giving you a crash course in 'Living and Loving West Texas.' I hope I'm not overwhelming you."

Cindy's hand rose to touch his cheek, as she had wanted to do that day on the way home from the Bistro. Here was the man she had met back in September. A man with strength and strong convictions.

"We had better get on with our tour."

Jimmy brushed a kiss across her lips. "The horse barns are down this way. As you can see, there are lots of additional barns, work areas, and storage sheds. With the dining room folks, we usually carry a full-time staff of fifteen employees."

By 9:00 the two of them, plus Dancer, were settled in one of the ranch pick-ups. They pulled back into the drive around noon.

During lunch Gramps asked if Cindy was tired. "I'm bushed from running to the truck." Everyone looked up, expecting details. "We covered a lot of territory; got out numerous times to look at something or talk to someone." Cindy began to laugh. "Then Dancer and I had to race back to the truck to see who could sit next to Jimmy. Now, he's so pleased with his popularity that Dancer and I can hardly stand him."

Gramps chuckled. "I need to get you down to the barn to match you with a horse. You ridden before?"

"Oh, my gosh! I never thought about that. How exciting. I've been on a horse, maybe two times, over the years. I'd love to try."

"Good. I'll turn you into a horsewoman in no time."

Gramps walked through the barn mumbling to himself and finally made his choice. "Let's try Blaze. She's of good temperament."

As Cindy watched them walk toward her, she was apprehensive. The horse dwarfed Gramps, but it was obvious who was in charge. Her comment was, "She's sure pretty, and BIG."

Gramps smiled. "You can handle it. Hold on to her halter while I round up the blanket, saddle, and bridle. She likes to be talked to."

Cindy could hear Gramps mumbling and chuckling to himself at the other end of the barn. "Well Blaze, that name sounds spunky to me. You seem like a gentle creature. You're not trying to fool me, are you?" The horse nuzzled her, and with that one simple movement, all was lost.

When Gramps got back he didn't have to ask any questions. It was obvious, this girl and Blaze would get along just dandy. "Here's a pick. I'll show you how to clean and check her hooves. Then you can brush her and comb her mane and tail."

Cindy gave him a surprised look. "I'm learning the ropes, right?"

"It's the only way. Lots to do before you get on a horse." Gramps taught her how to saddle up. After several tries she had the straps figured out. Then came the bridle. Finally, he stepped back. "Now, it's time to mount up." Cindy looked at him. "How do I get way up there?"

"There's a step. Lead your horse over here." Then, there sat Cindy Fillmore, on top of the world. She looked down on the kindly face of a patient old gentleman. They were both grinning; both sets of eyes were glistening with tears.

"Walk her around, Cindy. Sit proud, chin up. Keep talkin' to her."

After they had put everything away and brushed the horse down, Cindy and Gramps walked back to the house arm in arm.

Cindy went in to wash up and see if she could help with the meal.

Jimmy pulled Gramps aside. "How'd it go?"

"Blaze's mane, and that pretty hair of hers, is the same color. She sits up there mighty fine. Started out scared but it will come with lots of hard work. She'll love it if I can get her to relax and build her confidence.

"If you aren't interested in her, just let me know. I'd run off with her in a minute."

Hands in his pockets, shuffling dirt in the driveway, Jimmy appeared worried. "I know how you and Aunt Millie feel. Dad isn't saying much."

Gramps replied thoughtfully, "He's a cautious man. Has to think about things."

Cindy almost fell asleep at the table. They excused her early. What a day. No thinking this night.

She was still a bit weary in the morning. But she and Gramps went to the barn for a short while to work on some basics. A nap was necessary in the afternoon, as Jimmy had mentioned that they might go to the dance in town.

• • •

They were seated when the band started playing. The music made Cindy forget her weariness. You couldn't hide the fact that Jimmy was well known at these gatherings. He shook hands with everyone in the place, and Cindy was introduced to scores of people.

After watching the dancers, Cindy remarked, "My gosh, I'm not sure I can do these fast steps."

"You should have mentioned it before. I know where there's a dog that gives lessons." He laughed. "They're playing a slow number so let's start there."

Halfway through the song there was a shout that could be heard above the music. "Hey, Jimmy!"

"Hey, Taylor."

Cindy piped up. "Well now. More secrets? An assumed name, a mustache for disguise, and now an old girlfriend?"

"I like holding you in my arms and dancing," James said. "It feels good. But sometimes you talk too much." Cindy snuggled in closer and they finished the number.

Jimmy went 'round and brought two pops and a basket of popcorn to the table. He pulled his chair up close to Cindy's. "Taylor is Quincy Taylor. We were almost brought up together. We're like sister and brother. She's my best friend; well, was. Our relationship has always been very special to me. We will always be there for each other."

He looked deep into her eyes. "You mean the world to me, Cindy. Taylor is a lifelong friend. That's important to me, too. You must understand that."

Cindy never took her eyes from his. Although she didn't physically touch him, she felt like she was fully touching him, not only outside, but inside where his soul rested. "You are a remarkably honest man. My feelings for you are so deep and strong."

Jimmy stood and drew her to him. "I need to hold you. Let's dance, close." The music was slow, and inviting; the crowd on the floor seemed to dissolve.

When they returned to the table Cindy excused herself to go to the restroom. As she was washing her hands a girl, a bit smaller than herself, burst through the door. "So, you're his choice. Quincy Taylor's my name."

Cindy cocked her head and smiled. "Nice to meet you, Quincy. I'm Cindy Fillmore."

"No, please; never liked that one. Call me Taylor. It took Jimmy a spell, but he finally latched onto the right girl. The way you two look at one another, it will be a short engagement."

"Hold it. I think you are getting ahead of things. You don't know me at all. What makes you think I would be the right one?"

"Mark my word. I know Jimmy. You would never be here with him if he wasn't serious. And at the ranch over Thanksgiving, you mark my word."

Cindy took a deep breath and then let it out. "Do you read palms on the side?"

"I know Jimmy, trust me. We'll get to know each other better as time passes. If my prediction is right, you'll need me to run interference on one possible problem. Later we'll talk about that."

It was at this point that Cindy questioned why the two of them weren't interested in each other.

Taylor laughed. "Jimmy? He's a valued friend, but I am drawn to rough-and-tumble men when it gets past friendship. Oh, don't worry, I'm sure he's a passionate son of a gun with his woman of choice. But he and

I, naw. When it comes down to sink or swim, our relationship may be twined into even stronger rope than the marriage knot. I'd never thought about that before, but it might well be true."

After a few fast dances Cindy and James drove home in the moonlight. Cindy sat thinking. "Your friend Taylor. I like her. She's up front, doesn't waste words, comes right to the point. She's rather plain until she speaks, but there's something about her that's sexy, too. When she does say something she seems to be wise beyond her years in her thinking." Jimmy made no comment.

Between horseback riding and dancing, Cindy's legs felt like a two-day toothache.

Breakfast on Sunday was a leisurely affair. Aunt Millie turned to Cindy during a break in the conversation. "You have had an opportunity to get to know us a little bit over these few days. Share with us some information about your family."

"How embarrassing. I haven't even mentioned my mom. That's unforgivable. She's about it as far as family goes. My grandparents have been deceased for several years. My mom and I are very close. Although, I've been off on my own ever since college.

"Poor Mom. She's such a fine person. She's worked hard all her life. We get along great. She and my father were married four years. When she got pregnant, my father decided a child was not part of his agenda. He set up an adequate financial plan for my future. Then he left immediately. He started divorce proceedings right away. My mom was in shock. I don't believe her folks ever forgave him.

"The story I got was that she moved in with her folks for a month or so, then rented a very tiny apartment. From then on she was independent. I'm sure it was very difficult for her. I very seldom talk about this, and as I said it's hearsay. But since I'm on the subject would it be okay if I talk it through?"

Aunt Millie spoke up immediately. "If you would feel better by doing so, please continue. I was not meaning to pry."

"It just seems like I try not to think about it. When I do I like to go through the whole scenario in my mind, then put it back in storage. Does that sound odd?"

Jimmy took hold of her hand. They had talked about a lot of different things, but Cindy had kept this detail of her life locked away. Gramps and Sam sat with their heads lowered. Their desire to do or say something that would give relief to the moment was obvious, but it was just as plain that neither of them could think of what to do.

Aunt Millie came to the rescue again. "My dear, you go right ahead."

"As soon as the divorce was final my father moved to another state. An old friend of his told Mom that he had remarried. He married a lady who was interested in her career and not raising a family. There never was any further communication between them. I often wonder if he even knows that he has a daughter, not a son. Guess it doesn't matter. That would not have made a difference I'm sure.

"Mom said he liked his job, and a busy social life; and she thought he liked her, too. Their life had been good together. The two of them had not discussed having children. Their friends all had little ones. She had thought he would be pleased. She couldn't believe that he cared so little for her. He claimed that there was no question in his mind that the baby was his. The provisions he made took care of all my college needs. Up to that point my mom provided for me, not only financially, but with good care and an abundance of love.

"That's enough of that." Cindy slumped a little in her chair as though she had just been through an ordeal. She closed he eyes for a minute, then sat up and smiled. "I have had a good life; it's just that I wish the beginning had been different, especially for my mom.

"We have many friends but run a bit short on family. That's why these past days have been so special for me. You're family ties are so strong. It has been a delight to share with you. I appreciate your kindness."

Jimmy had released her hand several minutes ago. But in his mind he was holding her close and assuring her that she would never feel unloved again.

He stood up, indicating it was time to go. They had said their goodbyes to Dancer.

Cindy had dreaded the parting scene. They were gathered around the car. She walked up to Gramps and whispered in his ear, "Will you take care of Dancer?"

"You bet. I'll keep Blaze in good shape for you, too."

She went to shake Sam's hand. He held back just an instant; but it was long enough for her to notice. In a way it frightened her. Then he took her hand in both of his and quietly said, "We hope to see you again."

Cindy turned to Aunt Millie. They clung to each other for a moment. As they stepped apart Millie said, "You come back real soon. I'll miss having you around."

As they drove away, Aunt Millie turned and walked into the house.

The two men watched until they could see nothing but empty road. Gramps spoke first. "She sure seem like a keeper to me."

"She's a fine young woman. But will she be tough enough for the long haul, the hard times? You know what it's like out here. There are some rough things to handle. I would never stand in Jimmy's way, never. This weekend was not a true picture of what kind of life a rancher leads, not even one who runs a guest ranch. That's where my concern lies. But I must admit, she might be worth the challenge."

 CHAPTER 4

Over the noise of the old Ford, Jimmy could barely hear Cindy humming. Then she'd stop, and start again.

"I don't recognize the tune."

"It's new. I'm writing a ballad."

"Don't tell me you're a singer."

She laughed. "No, no. There will only be a single performance. But I'm not ready yet."

"Give me a drum roll when you are, okay?"

Cindy dug around in her purse and came up with a red ballpoint and a Mickey Mouse tablet. The miles rolled by. She finally let loose with a long drawn-out sigh. "I can't think of a tune that will work. It will have to be a reading instead. Here goes.

> *Miles and miles of stones and dust,*
>
> *Blown about by wind and trust.*
>
> *Smiles that cover tired faces.*
>
> *Mountains mixed with open spaces.*
>
> *Hired hands,*

Four-acred lands.

Millie with a heart of gold.

Gramps with stories still untold.

Sam, a man who's strong and bold,

A man of vision and of power,

Traveling through life, hour by hour.

Watching, planning, setting the pace,

You can't tell a thing by watching his face.

Taylor, with the sexy eyes.

Dancer was a big surprise.

Blaze-of-glory was the prize.

Then there's Jimmy, the juggler,

A smuggler, of sorts.

Introducing strangers to the scene,

He weaves the threads together,

Working them into a tapestry,

Depicting his love for west Texas.

Jimmy reached for Cindy's hand. He rubbed his thumb back and forth across her knuckles. "You're something else. Will you officially be my girl?"

Cindy smiled. "I might be able to manage that."

"We didn't fool you, did we? You saw through our painted picture of fun and frolic. You ignored our packaging and discovered a clear picture of how we function and work. There's a lot more to you than what one sees on the outside. That's what I like about you."

"Please tell me more about some of these people."

Jimmy commenced to tell the background of the people at the Pride Ranch and how they were woven together.

"Gramps is self-explanatory. You read my dad pretty well. Mother died when I was born. Aunt Millie and Fred were right there for Dad and me. They do have a little place of their own, but most of the time they're with us."

"LC is part Indian. The initials stand for Little Creek. I don't know the whole story, but he and my dad are very close. I can't remember a time when he wasn't around."

"If neither Dad nor I are available, he and Buc run the place. Buc is younger. But the three of them are a strong team. They can be tough, and hard to deal with."

"The Tylers are new. They packed up and left Montana so Randy, he's twenty-four, could rodeo. Our season is year-round, whereas the weather in Montana keeps the circuit short. Nice folks, good workers."

Jimmy remained quiet for a time, Cindy waited patiently. Finally, he remarked, "Taylor is a long and complicated story. That's better told in bits and pieces, over a period of time. You can't cover her in a few words. You will like her, I'm sure, but she is a puzzler. One thing, you have to accept her as she is."

• • •

The following morning, before classes, Cindy wrote a note to the folks at the ranch. Again she expressed her feelings about the visit. After thinking about it for awhile, she decided to address it to Aunt Millie, hoping that would be acceptable.

The days between their return to the university and the long Christmas break passed quickly. During this time it was decided that Jimmy would fly to Michigan after Christmas. The two of them would then fly back to school together on New Year's Eve day.

It was during the first week of December that Cindy wrote a second note to Aunt Millie, explaining the delivery of a special package and how to handle it.

She had some gifts wrapped for her mom and would finish that shopping after arriving in Michigan. All of a sudden she realized how good it would be to get home and spend time with her. My gosh, she missed her. She'd been busy and having a great time, but home was home, and Mom was Mom.

That was her family. Cindy could hardly wait.

That same evening, in Michigan, Leanna Fillmore sat in her warm robe and slippers. After the 11:00 news, she turned off the TV. Although she had watched it, she'd not heard a thing the newsman had said.

She sat thinking of Cindy's homecoming. Many letters had passed between them during the past months. Neither of them liked phone conversations. The woman who would arrive a few days before Christmas would be nothing like the girl who had left in mid-August.

Leanna had wrapped the pretty blue sweater with a cable design in festive paper just last night, awaiting the big day.

The phone rang, and it startled her because of the late hour.

"Hello."

"Mom, it's Cin. I miss you so and I'm anxious for the vacation to begin."

"Mental telepathy, or two great minds. Oh, Cindy! I was sitting here thinking the same thing." After a few more words they hung up.

A lady in one state and a young woman in another each reached for a box of tissues and had a good cry.

• • •

Leanna watched the plane circle, land, and taxi in. Everyone was watching for a face that would brighten their holidays.

Everyone could hear someone running. The first face was shining with a world-class smile and searching the crowd. Then Cindy spotted Leanna. They rushed toward one another and locked in an embrace.

Cindy was bubbling with news to share as they hurried to the car. The world was whole once more.

Leanna had to maintain her work schedule at the clothing store, but she and Cindy had plenty of time to spend together. They were like two college girls.

Cindy talked constantly about Jimmy and the ranch family. Leanna was anxious to hear it all.

Christmas morning they exchanged their numerous gifts. Then they went to see friends across town for a fine holiday meal.

• • •

After breakfast at the ranch there was the usual exchange of gifts. At the conclusion Aunt Millie announced, "I believe there is one more gift to be opened."

Jimmy said, "It's empty under the tree."

"This was a special delivery." She was gone from the room for a minute. Upon returning, she placed a large box in front of Jimmy.

He sat completely still. Then slowly he undid the mailing paper from the outside. The return address was Big Bend Saddlery. Inside was a hat box with a name stamped on the top: Custom Made Limpia Creek Hats.

Jimmy carefully lifted the lid. On top of the hat lay a hand-written note in a sealed envelope.

I know you'll have to break it in. You left your hat with me one night. You claimed it was part of you. In giving you this hat, I present you with my heart and soul.

Merry Christmas, My Love,

Cindy

Jimmy stood up saying, "If you will excuse me I think I need to take

Dancer for a walk."

After his departure Millie walked over to the box. She apologized but proceeded to read the private note. Then repeated it aloud.

Gramps was the first to speak. "I assume he is planning to make a move on this situation."

Millie replied, "Yesterday he showed me the engagement ring that he's taking to Michigan."

Sam remained quiet, but there was a smile of satisfaction on his face.

• • •

Jimmy drove back to school and then took a flight out from there.

He had not given Cindy a definite flight nor time of arrival. He wasn't sure how much of his time would be needed at the ranch. The arrangement was that he would take a cab from the airport.

Leanna's doorbell rang two days after Christmas. She opened the door to find a handsome young man standing on the porch. He removed his hat inquiring, "Mrs. Fillmore?"

She opened the door wide. "Mr. Pride, I believe. You are expected. Please come in. That's an impressive hat."

"It was a surprise Christmas gift from someone we both know."

Leanna explained that since Cindy had not known when he would arrive, she had gone visiting old friends. The two of them sat at the kitchen table talking over cups of coffee.

After a few minutes James turned very serious. "Since Cindy could arrive at any time, I would like to ask a favor. It's not polite so soon after my arrival, but would it be permissible for Cindy and me to have some time alone later this evening? If it's to your approval, I should like to ask your daughter to marry me, and I don't think I can stand another day without knowing her answer."

Leanna lay her hand on his. "I believe we can arrange it." She heard the garage door going up. Rising from her seat she said, "I need to go upstairs for a few minutes. She'll be happy to see you."

The front door opened and Cindy called out, "Sally was home, so I've been talking to her for the last hour and a half." By this time she was standing in the kitchen doorway.

The squeal of delight was heard on the second floor. After a few more minutes Leanna returned to the kitchen. "Well, Cin, I see you found your guest."

"Sin?" asked James.

"That's my home territory handle. C-I-N, silly! I owed you that."

After the evening news, Leanna said, "I'm reading a good book upstairs and I need to turn in early because of work tomorrow. See you two at breakfast."

She had dropped off to sleep when she heard the stairs being jumped two at a time. The door swung open. "Mom, Jimmy and I are going to be married! And, Mom, he said he wanted a family."

Leanna smiled as her head rested on the stacked-up pillows. "You knew, didn't you? Sneaks! That's what the two of you are." The door swung shut again and Cindy bounded back down the stairs.

Early the next morning Jimmy and Cindy called the ranch and received blessings from all.

When they departed on New Year's Eve day, Leanna gave each of them a big hug at the terminal. As she drove home she thought about all the lives that would be changed because of this marriage. The changes in her own life would be immense.

Maneuvering slushy roads, a chill attacked her spine and she shuddered. She gripped the steering wheel and proclaimed out loud, "Leanna, get hold of yourself. You're a big girl, it's adjustment time again. Transition, they say that's a woman thing."

She switched the radio on and began to sing along with the country tune. Obviously, Cindy had changed stations on her. The song was something about having gone country. Leanna laughed, life never ceased to come up with its little adventures.

 CHAPTER 5

It was evening when they deplaned and reclaimed their baggage. Jimmy arranged for a cab. "I left my car at your place. I thought that would work out."

After reaching the apartment Jimmy opened the trunk and deposited his things. He then proceeded up the stairs with Cindy's luggage. She used her backside to push the door closed. She set her other parcels on the floor.

"It's New Year's Eve, would you like to . . ."

"Party? No."

"Stay the night?"

"Let me change that to a definite yes. But I don't have any pajamas. They're down in the car."

Cindy walked over and snapped the bolt on the door. "Gee, that's too bad."

He looked so forlorn it was almost comical. Then his look changed and forlorn was not the look he was generating at all.

Cindy said, "I don't know about you, but I'm full of holiday food and I'm just plain tired."

Jimmy grinned and said, "I couldn't agree more."

"I do have a huge night shirt that would fit you."

"Okay."

Cindy heard the shower shut off and she opened the bathroom door just enough to toss the garment inside. When Jimmy came out he paraded around the room. "You didn't tell me that Winnie the Pooh and his friends would be sleeping over, too."

"Wait 'til you see my outfit." Minutes later she came out in her sleepers with the feet.

"Cindy, my love, come sit by me. We have much to talk about." Priorities got shuffled around and the discussion did not take place until after a big breakfast on New Year's Day. There were many questions, with few answers.

About 3:00, Jimmy stood. Pulling Cindy to him he gave her a quick kiss. "We've got to stay away from each other for a couple of days. I've got to zero in on my studies. There's a future to think about." He walked to the door, turned and walked back, kissed her again. "I've got to get out of here."

Cindy put her things away and organized her books and thoughts for the new semester. The holiday scene, her mom, getting engaged; exhaustion caught up with her.

She fell unto the bed. When her alarm sounded in the morning she was still in the same position. Dragging herself to class wasn't easy. Her whole life had changed since Thanksgiving, and this was just the beginning.

She smiled to herself. She was so fortunate. The future would be full of adjustments, hard work, and love.

After classes, she went home to study. The phone rang and she absentmindedly lifted the receiver. "Cindy here."

"You make life sound exciting."

"Had my nose in the books. Thought we weren't going to see each other for a few days."

"I can't see you. I said a couple of days, you say a few. Have you lost interest already?"

"So, what is your new plan, James?"

After spitting a few more words back and forth they decided to meet on mutual ground, at the park. When Cindy spotted him she ran the rest of the way, linking her arm with his. "Jimmy, was that our first spat?"

"Whatever it was, I didn't like it. Marry me today."

"It's not that easy. How does July sound?" He looked so dejected she felt sorry for him.

"All the fuss and muss goes with the program. We'll try to keep it as painless as possible." After a few days each adjusted to the new turn his and her life had taken.

 CHAPTER 6

The list of things to do grew to large proportions. It started out reasonable. It was the details that added up.

- *wedding preparations*

- *a teaching job*

- *a place to live*

- *finish studies*

- *don't forget Dancer*

- *be pleasant*

- *etc.*

This note hung on Cindy's refrigerator.

It was mid-February before they headed for the ranch again. Cindy sat with a yellow pad on her lap, writing down questions about things she had to work out. "I can't be a guest at the ranch anymore. This time I need to work right along with the others."

As the car pulled in, Gramps was putting Dancer through her paces on the training schedule. When the car doors opened and Dancer spotted the occupants, Gramps didn't have the heart to make her sit.

It became a circus with Dancer as the main event in the center ring. In minutes the crowd grew larger. Everyone was hugging Cindy and shaking hands with Jimmy.

Finally, the fracas quieted. Cindy knew it would be a tiring weekend. She hated to disrupt the busy routine, but there were some important facts that had to be straightened out.

After lunch Sam took them to his office. "So, how are the plans coming?"

"We'd like to aim for early July. I'm trying to figure out how to get you all to Michigan."

Sam remained quiet for a few minutes, then rubbed his chin with his fingers. "You know, it's impossible for all of us to come your way. I have a suggestion. For years we've had a rodeo and celebration here at the ranch on the 4th. Suppose you have the wedding here.

"We could combine the two. By no means would I want to take away the seriousness of your wedding. But maybe we could figure a way to knit it together; maintaining dignity, and combining it with fun. A shindig with class."

You could almost see the wheels meshing in Cindy's head. "You know, I always said that if I got married I'd like it to be different, memorable. That would sure do the trick." And she laughed.

Sam continued, "I thought if it's okay with you, I'd keep that week before the wedding free. That way your friends from Michigan could use this as a vacation if it fitted into their schedules.

"They could ride the horses, eat their meals in the cafeteria, and enjoy the cabins. Everything is here for the reception. Our girls can do a fine job for you.

"I could set up some excursions in the area. We have the perfect facility."

"It sounds like a dream, but Sam, my friends don't have that kind of money. And for my mother to pay for all that would be out of the question.

It sounds like movie material."

Sam moved forward in his chair and took both of her hands in his. "Did you think I would charge?"

"Oh, Sam, you can't do all that. My mom would not be happy with such an arrangement."

It was left that Cindy should think on it before she said no. Jimmy had said nothing. Later, he told her that he was as surprised as she. Such extravagance. But it sure sounded like a whoppin' good time. He kind of liked the idea. His dad had thought about this in great detail. But this had to be Cindy's decision. It sounded like a good solution to him. Jimmy left to help repair some fences.

Cindy walked through the kitchen and paused to talk about Sam's idea. Millie thought it would be great. Cindy then left the house behind and began to meander through the barns, with Dancer at her side. Sitting on the fence around the corral, she noticed a rider approaching.

Taylor dismounted. Cindy climbed down from her perch stating, "Boy am I glad to see you. I need to talk."

"Shoot."

"Sam has suggested the wedding be here. It would be spectacular. He wants to pay for everything."

"Sounds good to me. What's the holdup? Sam likes you a lot. He wants you and Jimmy to be happy."

"Money doesn't buy happiness."

"You think he don't know that? It doesn't buy life either, or Jimmy's mom would be here sharin' this time with you, instead of me.

"No way the rancher friends from here could attend if it was in your territory. It would be extremely difficult even for the family."

Taylor looked around to make sure no one could overhear. "Besides, Sam needs a boost. He's been alone too long. His offer is genuine and from the heart. Make him happy. He needs to think of something besides work. I think he'd love every bit of it."

She grinned. "He needs some lovin'. He's the nicest man I've ever known. He's sort of like a glue factory, holds everything together."

"You people out here are all prejudiced. What if I voted no?"

"Suit yourself. I'd give it a big yes. Sam's a shrewd businessman, but he's got a big heart. Don't break it. Respect him, and he'd do anything for you two."

Cindy questioned why Taylor had shown up when she did. Taylor explained, "I could feel your S.O.S. Let's go riding, get your mind on something else. Scramble the worry pattern. Saddle Blaze."

So, off they went. The ride helped clear Cindy's head. Quincy Taylor, an extraordinary friend.

"Taylor, would you consider being in the wedding?"

Taylor's horse was reined in so fast that Cindy had to jerk Blaze sideways or there would have been a collision. "There won't be one if that happens again. Remember, I'm not as experienced as you."

"No one ever asked me to do anything like that before."

"Well, how about it?"

"Darned if I won't."

They rode the rest of the way in silence. Cindy was curious about this girl who tried so hard to help others. Was anyone watching over her?

After returning to the house Cindy knocked softly on the study door. "Come in."

"Well, I guess you win. I'm concerned about my mom's reaction to all this."

"She and I can work it out. Don't let that be your worry. You plan it and I'll be glad to help in any way I can. "

In the early morning she and Jimmy went out to pay a visit to Buffer. The truck topped the hill and Jimmy got out, giving a shrill whistle. Over a nearby hill, running full speed, came the most beautiful horse Cindy had ever laid eyes on. As he gained on the truck she realized how powerful he must be.

He pulled up next to Jimmy, snorted, and pawed the ground. "Come 'round on the other side of the cab, fella, and meet a very special lady."

Cindy whispered, "Do I dare get out?"

"Don't let his size fool you. He's like an old teddy bear."

They produced a magnificent silhouette. A man, his pick-up truck, his horse, and his woman. He had it all. Jimmy swung Cindy off her feet and twirled her around. He gave Buffer's hindquarter a swat with his hand and the horse took off on a run. They climbed back in the truck.

Jimmy sat quietly with his hands on the steering wheel. "It's all I've ever wanted: the land, a truck, my horse, and my woman. I'm glad you want to be a part of my plan."

"Don't know as I like bein' last," she said as she nudged him in the side.

Jimmy gave her a devilish look and with one quick move had her pinned to the seat. He was kissing her so hard, she could barely breathe. As he moved away from her, he started the motor.

"Is that what wranglers do, get a girl out in the middle of nowhere and corner her?"

"You liked it, and don't tell me different. You weren't fighting me."

"Well, shame on me." With that she straightened her blouse. "You're a scoundrel; please, don't change."

As soon as they returned to the ranch they packed up and headed for school.

Cindy dreaded calling her mom, but postponing the news would not improve matters. Her mom was hesitant, but she did understand. They both had to admit that it did sound reasonable, and exciting. But the financial arrangement pricked her pride, as Cindy predicted. The conversation ended with her assuring Cindy that it would iron out. Not to worry.

 CHAPTER 7

The end of March marked another trip to the ranch. Friday night Sam took them into a nearby town for supper. During the meal Cindy learned about the different films that had been made in the area. *Giant* with James Dean and Rock Hudson was the best known. Jimmy and Sam approached Cindy about her thoughts for the rehearsal dinner. Choices were limited. She was delighted that their top choice was here, where they had just finished a very tasty meal. Arrangements were made on the spot.

Saturday morning Cindy called the number in the phone book listed under the school superintendent's office. She explained her situation and inquired about the superintendent's name and if it might be possible to contact him.

On the other end of the line, Mr. Hornsby smiled and informed her that he would be working in his office for another hour. If she'd care to stop in, he'd like to meet her. According to rumors, he had been expecting her.

Cindy quickly changed her clothes. Borrowing one of the ranch vehicles, she drove into town. Observing the grounds and hallways of the school, Cindy was impressed that it appeared to be a well-run school system.

She left the building in high spirits: a fourth-grade teacher was retiring. Mr. Hornsby said that he would like to have a new person with innovative ideas.

Cindy couldn't help but respect the educator, even though his hair was shaggy and his shoes scuffed. You could tell he was totally absorbed in this little school system.

He promised to check with the board and notify her with results. She had met the requirements for teaching in Texas.

While in town, Cindy stopped at the restaurant where Taylor worked. She had a cup of coffee while Taylor finished with a customer.

Looking around, Cindy checked the food delivered to the few occupied tables: it smelled great and the servings were substantial. The curtains were faded and worn, with hems unraveling; and they were so out of kilter that it looked like a design. The chairs had red plastic coverings; many had splits where the stuffing was working its way out to the daylight. It appeared to have been obtained by squatter's right, and nothing much had improved.

But all the faces were smiling and the place had a friendly, down-home feel.

Taylor had told her that she had begun working here while in high school; she just couldn't seem to walk away from the place. It provided her with her needs. More than that, the owners were like family. Everyone who came in the place knew her. She was as much a fixture as the old-fashioned cash register sitting on the glass case by the front door.

Looking at her reminded Cindy of a lost orphan. It seemed as though she deserved more. Jimmy had been right: a strong friendship was forming between the two.

There was a break before the lunch rush, so Taylor joined her with a mug of coffee and rhubarb pie for each.

Cindy had sent ahead the pattern and material. A local person was to sew Taylor's dress. Cindy could tell she was excited about being part of the wedding.

Cindy inquired about a wedding cake. Taylor suggested a lady from their kitchen who did that out of her home. "They really are nice. Better get a chocolate groom's cake; that's Jimmy's favorite." They persuaded the woman to join them for coffee and discussed the cake order.

After returning to the ranch, Cindy spent more than an hour with the cook setting up the hearty reception meal.

• • •

At the beginning of April a pre-invitation was sent to guests who would be traveling a long distance. They would have to make more detailed plans. Cindy hoped that Sam would not be disappointed. The whole picture sounded appealing to her.

She felt that such an arrangement would make it possible for some friends to attend who otherwise wouldn't have considered it.

You are invited to a Shindig to celebrate the marriage of

Cindy Fillmore and James Pride.

(Formal invitation will arrive at the appropriate time)

*Shindig - n 1 a: a social gathering with dancing b: a large or lavish party
2: celebration*

*The Shindig will be in the big State of Texas on the groom's family Guest Ranch.
Not only will they be hosting the party BUT they have opened their ranch for
additional activities the week prior to the big event.*

THE PRIDES SAY "COME ON YOU CITY SLICKERS"

****** YES -free of Charge- YES *******

*Bring your family and stay in the guest cabins. They will be open to you from
noon on Saturday, July 5, 1997, until noon on Sunday, July 13. Three meals a
day will be provided at the Pride Ranch cafeteria.*

ACTIVITIES

Rodeo - Tours - Horseback riding - Talk to "real" cowboys

Experience ranch life firsthand - relax - have fun

ETC., ETC., ETC.

*That's why the advance and special notice, so you can plan ahead. Spend your
vacation with us. Questions? Need Details? Make Reservations.*

Contact: Pride Ranch

P.O. Box 8
«Attention Wedding»

Tango, Texas

80808-1234

1-555-800-8008

R.S.V.P. as soon as possible.

 ## CHAPTER 8

The end of April was the last time Cindy Fillmore visited the ranch before July. It was a busy few days. Cindy had signed her school contract, and she and James had rented a tiny place in town. Jimmy would move in as soon as he got home from school.

She had forgotten about the flowers. Ordering those allowed her to scratch one more chore from her list.

They had talked to the minister on one of their previous visits. This Saturday they were invited to have lunch with him.

That evening as the family sat around the ranch table Cindy made a comment. "My friends back home are asking me why someone out here was trying to secede from the union?"

Sam pushed his chair back from the table. "I don't know the answer, except to say there are people like that around the globe. It's sad and I don't understand. I think their brains are like an overripe watermelon, all mush inside." That's all that was said.

The most novel happening had been meeting Big John. Jimmy had talked about him time and again. He referred to him as "our local lion hunter."

Cindy had pictured him just as Jimmy had wanted her to. What else, but a big brute of a man. In her mind she had exaggerated and made him so strong that he could strike the cat with such a blow that he would have killed it instantly.

When they arrived at his place, his petite wife Lila and toddler met them at the door. Coming across the yard was a tall skinny man. Cindy looked at Jimmy, who was doubled over with laughter. She'd been had again.

Cindy found out she would be teaching in the same building where Lila worked, so she'd know someone on the staff. She knew the month of August would be spent preparing her classroom and tentative class schedule.

It was the toddler's time for bed. After that routine, Jimmy and Big John began reminiscing about their younger days.

Jimmy got things rolling by speaking about Jake, John's elderly neighbor. "I remember back in high school when you and Jake and his hounds would go out at night."

"I've been hunting lions and black bears, on my own, for about seven years now. Most of my hounds are registered Blueticks, but I have one Redtick and a Bluetick Walker cross. The Bluetick seems to be a colder nose: they can smell an older track, and can track in tougher conditions."

Cindy was fascinated with all this information. The conversation jumped from dogs to children to teaching, but it always returned to hounds.

"At three months, I start with basic discipline; at six or eight months they start going with my older dogs. I've got one six-month-old that has already seen four lions and is doing quite well. They are three or four years old before they are completely trained. They have to work for their feed."

Jimmy spoke up again. "John has a master's in wildlife biology; he handles our range and wildlife management. I don't know what we'd do without him."

Cindy posed the question, "Lila, how do you feel about all this?"

"We used to work with troubled boys and sometimes John would be unavailable. Some nights I'd take the dogs out hunting by myself. I enjoy it. That was before the baby."

"Well, now, I can see that I've got to toughen up to live out here in the wilds." Everyone laughed, but Cindy was serious. She knew she had a lot to learn.

• • •

The following day Cindy and James spent time in the yard with Dancer. "Jimmy, you look spooked. You okay?"

"Haven't you heard the old saying, 'Cowboys don't sleep much, you can do that when you die.'"

Cindy felt like she was going to cry. She must have looked it, too. Instantly, Jimmy was by her side.

"It's supposed to be funny."

"I guess we are both overly tired. Will life ever seem normal? Oh, Jimmy, let's go back to the apartment."

They'd had a swell visit and now Cindy had some new friends in Texas.

 CHAPTER 9

On the way back to school, the motion of the car was making Cindy drowsy. Jimmy switched the radio off and began talking in a low tone, as if to himself. Cindy caught the word Taylor and was immediately alert. The more her and Taylor's friendship increased, the less she seem to know about the girl.

"I guess the two families were reasonably close. Our birthdays are within the same month. After my mother died the Taylors came by a lot. Taylor and I shared teething rings. People said we rolled around on the floor like puppies. We ran through the barnyards and pushed each other into mud puddles; got into lots of mischief. We were just two little people who always got along and always had loads of fun romping through life.

"One Sunday she and her folks came to church and I didn't think it was her. Her mom had taken her to the parlor and gotten her hair fixed up. She had on a white dress, lacy socks, white shiny shoes, and a pretty white hat. All that white made the freckles on her nose and face stand out like they were painted on. She was a girl. Her eyes sparkled and she laughed when she saw the shocked look on my face. I wouldn't go near her.

"Next time they came around she had on her play clothes, but it was never quite the same. She was as unruly as ever. Even though we were just youngsters, I felt like I should look after her. She didn't like that one bit. I got shoved down quite a few times before I got it through my head that she was really the same as she had been. Finally, it worked itself out. The realization was that we were there for each other if need be. It was an unspoken commitment.

"When her dad died we were in our early teens. At first, her mother seemed to adjust to the situation.

"It was then that Quincy began to discover that she was a female and she became hard to handle. Mrs. Taylor couldn't control the problems of her daughter's growing-up years. No one was sure who created the undercurrent, the mother or the daughter."

Cindy felt that maybe this explained some things. Taylor very seldom revealed anything about her past. Often she seemed to be smoldering inside; jumpy, as if she would erupt.

"Has she ever used drugs, Jimmy? Sometimes she reminds me of a wild horse that has been driven into a corral. Like she wants to break and run, but is afraid to. Occasionally, her eyes have the look of a very frightened animal that has been caged."

"She's never messed with stuff like that. There's just something boiling inside and it needs to be capped.

"She and her horse Lightning enter contests and races at the fairs and rodeos. No one can beat them. It's like she's on fire. The fire rages inside, down deep. Don't know if anyone will ever be able to calm her down. Thank goodness that side of her is under control most of the time.

"She's crazy about Parker Bates. You'll see him around. Handsome cuss. As dangerous as they come. He likes her a lot, when he's with her. When he's not he likes whoever he's with. He couldn't care less. She knows, acts like it's no big deal, but it hurts. That's one thing she refuses to talk to me about. She knows my advice."

Cindy commented, "When we first met she said something about having to run interference for me, but never explained."

Jimmy thought for a while. "Her mother has turned mean and nasty the last few years. Some folks say that after Mr. Taylor died she got it in her mind that Taylor and I would marry. Or maybe my dad would get interested in her and that one way and another the two families would become one.

"My dad has never trusted her for some reason. He's polite, for old times' sake, but that's the extent of it. He's asked a few ladies in the county out, but nothing seems to come of it."

Cindy was shocked with this information. It made her apprehensive. The pairing of Jimmy and her had seemed to make everyone happy. An altercation about the wedding had never entered her thoughts. She was visibly shaken.

Jimmy reached for her hand. "Hey, woman, nothing is going to plow us under. Not even the Wicked Witch of the West. Love conquers all, my lovely Cindy. Smile for me."

Cindy's smile was weak. These facts would not be easily forgotten. She had met Mrs. Taylor and remembered her look of disapproval.

"How long has Taylor been out on her own?"

"She moved into her trailer when she was halfway through her senior year. Said it was getting unbearable at home. I offered to help with finances, but she wouldn't have it. She'd saved her tip money from work until she had enough for a month's rent. Pickin's were slim, but she refused any offer of help. Not as a female, but as a person, I love her and would do anything to help her."

Now Cindy could see some of the puzzle pieces of Taylor's life and how they fitted together. The picture on the top of the box was not a happy one.

• • •

Cindy and James had set aside the first two weeks in May for themselves. Classes and each other; no wedding plans. They went to the movies and for walks and dreamed of their future together.

During the middle of May they each went home. The last thing Jimmy said to Cindy was, "I'll be glad when this wedding is over. I want you to be my lawfully wedded wife."

Cindy's reply was, "I think it's a testing period. If you can survive these complicated preparations, you can get through most of life's trials. It won't be long now, James."

There was reluctance in their parting. But these few weeks had their purpose also: the last time they would spend with their families as single individuals. It would never be the same again. They would step into a new life.

 CHAPTER 10

The last two weeks in May were gone in a flash. June seemed like an eternity. Cindy swore that each day was longer than the previous one.

Thank goodness mail didn't travel by Pony Express anymore. Cindy would have been responsible for a lot of broken-down horses.

Detailed plans traveled on the miles of telephone wires that stretched between Michigan and Texas.

Dresses were finished, packed carefully, and sent ahead. Two of Cindy's girlfriends from Michigan, and Quincy Taylor, would be bridesmaids.

The wedding invitations were handed to the friendly face behind the counter at the post office on June 10th.

Leanna Fillmore and Samuel James Pride
request your presence at the marriage of their children

Cindy Fillmore

And

James Samuel Pride

On Saturday July twelve, Nineteen hundred and ninety seven at one o'clock in the afternoon

First United Methodist Church
Tango, Texas
Reception to follow at the Pride Ranch

Cindy sat on a lawn chair in her mom's back yard, enjoying the variety of flowers on the bank. Her mother spent hours pulling weeds and tending the display of color. Herbs were a favorite. Among them were lemon balm and spearmint. Leanna served her iced tea with mint in the glass and lemon slices. Every year she tried to grow lavender but was never successful.

Leanna claimed that she lacked a green thumb, but Cindy didn't agree. Leanna's only complaint was that it was a job that was never finished.

As she rested there, Cindy's mind wandered to Texas, remembering the saying, "You judge a man by the horse he rides." She closed her eyes and pictured Jimmy riding Buffer across the open land. They looked strong and free. She hoped her entering the picture would never take that look of freedom from them.

• • •

Jimmy was putting in long hours at the ranch. He had decided to continue to keep Dancer out there for the time being. Although not a typical ranch dog, she had adjusted well to the surroundings. Gramps said, "Don't tell her she's not a hound. She'll never know the difference."

Jimmy did not tell Cindy how many nights he got home well after dark, covered with dust and dirt ground into his skin, hair, and clothes.

Some nights he would walk through the door of the little rented house without turning on any lights. He'd collapse in his favorite chair. He'd tossed a ragged sheet haphazardly over it, hoping it wouldn't get in worse shape than it was already.

Other nights he'd throw his body across the bed, boots and all. He'd not bothered to make it up. Before the ancient springs stopped squeaking he'd be sound asleep.

Mornings he'd get up before dawn, take a shower, put on clean clothes, gulp a quick cup of strong black coffee, and head out the door. For lunch and supper he joined the others at the ranch.

Aunt Millie continued to do his wash. She'd throw his garments in the machine and run them through a rinse cycle first to rid the material of the filth. While the washer was running, she'd fix breakfast for Sam, Jimmy, Gramps, and her Fred.

One morning Millie cornered Sam and voiced her concern about the boy. She was not happy with his response.

"Now, Millie, he's a grown man. There's lots of work to be done. He's doing more than his share, but someday this will be his ranch."

She snapped back, "That sounds cold and calculating. He looks unkempt. Doesn't shave half the time. It's not like him."

"Undoubtedly, he misses Cindy." With that he produced a half-smile.

"I'm beginning to think Fred is right, neither of you knows about love and happiness anymore. If you two don't learn to live a little, this place will eat you alive."

The following morning Millie continued where she left off the day before, as if no time had elapsed. She grumbled through the frying of the bacon and the stirring of the scrambled eggs. Finally, she laid aside the two-pronged fork and the wooden spoon, and turning toward the four of them, she exploded.

"The only one of you with any spunk is Gramps. Sam and Jimmy are running a race to see who can fall on his face first. You are both moping around. Can't stand either one of you. When Cindy gets here she's going to shake the puddin' out of you two. Maybe we can have a funeral before the wedding. I'll be glad when she arrives. I'm darned tired. Fred and I aren't getting any younger and I want to spend more time with him." With that she drew her apron to cover her face and began to cry.

The four men looked stunned. Gramps reached for his hat and quietly left the house. Fred rushed to Millie's side and put his arms around her. That, in itself, was a gesture never seen before. Millie and Fred had always kept their displays of affection very private.

Sam's and Jimmy's thoughts were identical. This woman had acted as a combination mother, wife, sister, and aunt for years. She cleaned their house, cooked and washed, and worried about them. She'd been their nurse and listened to their woes. They each felt sick and ashamed.

Fred kissed her and smoothed back her hair, then he left to do his chores. Millie turned away.

Turning back, she was still sniffling, but she started in again.

"It isn't as if you don't have plenty of help around here. The two of you act like this place can't function without your constant supervision. The staff that works here is like family. I'd trust any of them with my life. They are devoted to the ranch, everyone and everything connected with it. Care for people, care for each other. Take a day off. Go look at a horse, buy a new pair of boots, or some other foolish thing. Enjoy yourselves. You've both been awful lately. If you act like this when that lovely young lady gets here I'll have your hide."

Sam put up his hand gesturing for her to stop. Then he turned to his son.

"Well, we have our instructions for the day. Are you about ready to go?"

It was the first time Jimmy had felt lighthearted in weeks. "You bet."

Turning to Millie, Sam said, "My instructions for today are this: you and Fred be out of here when we return this evening. There's plenty of time before the wedding people roll in. I don't want to see you two for a week. Go home to your place, go on vacation, whatever. Okay?"

Millie's sad face turned to a smile. "I guess we're all uptight with this big affair in the making."

Sam and Jimmy's first stop was the florist in a nearby town. A dozen roses were to be delivered to Pride Ranch, as soon as possible. A card would not be necessary.

They returned early in the evening just as Fred and Millie were going to climb into their pick-up. Millie was clutching her roses. The atmosphere was totally void of the morning's stress.

"A young lady called from Michigan. We had quite a visit. She wondered if her intended still intended to. She was afraid he had changed his mind."

Jimmy's smile vanished. "Aunt Millie, I love that girl so much I can't stand it. I hate that little house without her in it. I need her with me. She's my sunshine. She's my world. I thought if I worked 'til I dropped, then I'd just pass out at night time and the loneliness wouldn't be so painful. Life isn't worth a lucky horseshoe without her."

"Tell her that, not me. But, Jimmy, you have to be yourself first, then you can be a husband. You can't be one without the other. That's important for survival."

Jimmy winked. "I've got a phone call to make." And he started toward his car.

Sam removed his hat and stood facing his sister. "Thanks, Mil."

"You haven't called me that since we were kids."

"I never really sat down with you and Fred and thanked you properly for all the wonderful things you've done for Jimmy and me. You've kept us alive."

As they drove away Millie waved out the window. "See you next week."

• • •

At long last, July 1st arrived. The Amtrak train pulled away from the local depot with two very excited ladies on board.

There was the wait from noon until evening in the Chicago station. That was entertaining in itself.

Then they boarded the sleeper car, heading for Texas. Things were running late, so they decided against supper.

The nice assistant turned the seats into berths, and the fun started. They were so tired they were silly. As convenient as the arrangements were, they were confining when it came to two women trying to get organized. They both fell asleep instantly. This trip had been a long time coming.

At 2:30 in the morning each realized that the other was awake. For an hour or so they watched the lights of the countryside and small towns. Then there was a big city. Where were they? Climbing back in their berths, each slept soundly until daylight.

Then there was the shifting. "You stand here, I'll move there." They dealt with the tiny sink, and the adjustable function of the shower. Then they were ready to face the world, and they headed for the dining car.

Move fast, hand on to the backs of seats, try not to fall in anyone's lap was the best advice.

They were seated with two young boys. One was a black kid traveling with his grandmother, who had remained in coach. They were on their way to see his dad. The other was a few years older. His first statement was, "What nationality are you? I'm Italian." He was traveling by himself on his way to his grandparents. He told Leanna and Cindy that if they traveled through Chicago again and had such a long layover that they must come to his neighborhood. Just around the corner from where he lived they would find the best Italian restaurant in Chicago. What a joy the two were, both talkative, and each impressed them. The world would be in good hands in the future after all.

Leanna chose her favorite, French toast. It was delicious. The sleeper tickets included the three meals each day.

Returning to their compartment, they discovered that the kind assistant had converted their bedroom back to a comfortable sitting room.

Gradually, the scenery changed. Neither of them had traveled by train before and found it a pleasant means of getting from one place to another.

The dining car seating was the most fun of all. There was the Oriental businessman and his wife. At one time they had lived in California. Once a year he traveled back there to visit friends. While there he would purchase used semi-truck beds and cabs. They were then shipped to his country, where they were restored to fine working condition and resold. At supper time, they sat with a man who used to be a supplier of records for the Wurlitzer juke boxes.

In between the meals and chit-chat Leanna realized that with each momentum of the wheels she was losing her daughter. Not yet, but closer, closer, closer. It saddened her. But life moves on; the same as the train cars, passing so quickly you can't count them.

"Cindy, your courtship, or whatever they call it these days, has been like a fairy tale. Are you ready for when the last page of the fable says, The End?"

Cindy smiled. "Is this our Mother-Daughter talk?" Leanna laughed at that. "No, but some of the most intelligent brides neglect to admit that reality will strike sometime. He'll work long hard hours, you'll be teaching. The snuggling will seem to disappear. It will seem like love has slipped away. It's not so, but the feelings take on a different dimension. The adjustment is not a simple one. There're disappointments, sometimes cruel attitudes. Marriage is a tough challenge, but it is rewarding. The changes are hard to understand. The most difficult thing to remember is the other person. It is human nature to think about your own feelings first.

"By now you're thinking, how would she know? Eyes and ears open, and passing years. I wish you love, you must know that. Life does not provide guarantees."

They both remained quiet and the sway of the train allowed them each a relaxing short nap.

One more night, by noon tomorrow, Leanna knew that arriving at the station in Texas would be the same as the wedding ceremony. As they would get off the train the conductor might as well call out, "Who gives this woman to this man? And also his family?" She must then relinquish her connection to this child. She had read somewhere that children are only on loan. How true.

Leanna stood, saying, "I'm going to the snack bar and buy something devilish that I shouldn't have."

Cindy sat by herself, contemplating her future. She also knew what her mother must be feeling.

When the train crossed the line into Texas, Leanna's bubble really burst. Cindy was a walking information booth.

"Wait 'til you meet Sam. He solves all problems. He's the kind of person you want to lean on. You'll love him." She seemed to be as taken with the father, and his superhuman abilities, as she was with his son.

"In '96 the area was so drought-stricken, it cost the farmers and ranchers billions of dollars. They have low humidity, abundant sun, and clear skies. Sometimes there are heavy rainfalls. Due to the steep and rocky terrain, it produces flooding. Sometimes there are thunderstorms but rain doesn't reach the ground due to evaporation. Three weeks after the first rain, usually in July, things get green." She took a breath.

Leanna could see that that was not the end of the spiel.

"Because of the lack of dependable moisture it takes 40 to 90 acres to feed one cow. Ranching is a gamble. That's the reason so many ranchers have switched over to running a guest ranch."

"The cow is the factory, the calf the product. Have I forgotten anything? Oh, yes, in ranch talk one square mile is a section."

"Hey, kid, are you trying to sell me Texas?"

"I won't have to. You'll see."

Leanna glanced out the window and said, "What is that?"

"Oh, that's a Javelina. Turn the J to an H. It looks like a wild pig. There're different stories. Some say it's not in the pig family at all. Some say it's totally useless. Others say, if you pen it and feed it grain then the meat is good. One thing everyone agrees on. It is destructive."

Cindy began to fidget. Leanna suggested rounding things up, as the map indicated theirs would be the next stop.

• • •

Leanna had spotted Jimmy, and they waved to one another.

Cindy almost knocked the conductor over as he was setting the step on stones for people to alight safely. She hurdled some luggage and was in the center of waiting arms quicker than Leanna could blink. Leanna felt a bolt of pure happiness pass through her heart. The train men were all smiling. "Looks like the feeling is mutual."

Leanna had been so busy watching the happy reunion that she hadn't noticed the men piling up the luggage away from the track. She turned to them. "The wedding is the 12th." The three men cheered. She handed each of them a $20 bill.

"No, ma'am, we can't accept that much."

"Think of us on that day and have a party of your own. This was a special trip. There will never again be another two days like these last two. We appreciate your many acts of kindness. Have a safe trip home." She walked over to the kids.

"Break it up, you two. Let's get this stuff moved. I need to use the restroom in the station." She knew it was excitement and nervousness that was pushing her toward the bathroom.

"We'll get these things in the van. Dad is somewhere around. I think he ran into someone he knew."

Leanna's glance brought into focus two men conversing further down the track. They separated, the huge cumbersome one headed her way. Stepping inside the building she saw a slender sickly looking fellow coming from the men's room.

The sign for the ladies was barely readable, hanging from one bent rusty nail. Many uncertainties were whirling through her head.

Sam had been dealing with an upset stomach since breakfast. He very seldom suffered such distress. As he stepped out of the gent's room he nearly ran into a slender woman in her fifties who had definitely had one too many cocktails. Moving past her his thoughts were, Oh please, I hope that's not her.

He was standing on the platform looking about when he heard a light footstep behind him. As he turned partway around, he observed a fine-looking woman who appeared to be searching for a familiar face.

"Are you . . . ?"

"Could you by chance be . . . ?"

"Sam Pride."

"Leanna Fillmore." With that Leanna linked arms with Sam. She looked up at him with a sigh of relief; sparkling eyes and a questioning smile. "Are you as scared as I am? This is the first time I've been able to admit that even to myself."

Sam patted the arm linked with his. "We'll get through it together."

When they rounded the corner of the station the kids were settled, close together, in the back seat. "So, you guys found each other? Guess we were too busy to miss you."

 CHAPTER 11

Within a half an hour they were at the front gate. Sam pulled up by the ranch house long enough to introduce Gramps and Millie to Leanna. Up the hill was cabin #28. Everyone unloaded the van hurriedly. Something was said about, after she had rested, to come down to the office area. There was the noise of the van's tires moving the gravel in the roadway as it disappeared in a cloud of dust.

There stood Leanna: a cabin key in one hand, the ranch brochure and map in the other. She was surrounded by an eerie silence. It was as if she had been dropped off on another planet, where no civilization existed. Isolation could be a pleasant situation, if it was by choice. What was this? Was the mother of the bride that dispensable? Maybe she was like Alice and had fallen down a rabbit hole.

The stillness carried a heaviness with it. It was frightening, like it was pressing in on her. It made her feel like her air intake was being regulated, like her breathing should be shallow; almost as if she should tiptoe when moving about.

Leanna had the sensation that the world, as she knew it, had dropped away. Walking inside the cabin she checked her face in the bathroom mirror. She didn't appear older than yesterday. She was wondering why everyone took it for granted she needed a nap. Well, come to think of it, it didn't seem like such a bad idea.

She sat down in the large sturdy rocking chair; she slipped her feet out of her shoes and propped them up on one of the suitcases. A window was pushed up to let in the fresh air and she heard the leaves rustle on a nearby tree.

There was the pile of luggage and boxes that had arrived earlier. Two double beds, a round table, the nice bathroom, and plenty of windows. The colors and furniture produced a cozy down-home atmosphere. It was going to be a fine place for her stay.

Guess the sudden being alone had thrown her into a panic. She had been accustomed to being alone before mid-May. From then until now had been very different. She hadn't realized how she had missed the rush of activities, of being constantly on the go.

She had allowed herself to become an old woman, beyond her years, without knowing it. She thought she was busy. But she had become inactive in the things that kept her young.

There would be some changes made when she returned home. She'd get involved in some new creative projects.

Her routine was too highly organized, no pizzazz in it. When Cindy had been home that six weeks, there had been surprises, motivation, life.

For twenty-some years she had lassoed herself with an imaginary rope of responsibilities. Her mind was racing with enthusiasm. It was time to break loose.

Her life had slid into a mundane pattern. Shame on me, she thought. It was then that she began to appreciate this down time. It had opened her eyes.

Immediately ahead was almost two weeks of new territory, new people. She'd be caught up in a wedding; a shindig, to beat all. Then she would travel back home on the train; and she would experience things and feelings that would be new to her.

She was about ready to jump out of the rocker, to get started on this adventure, when she felt the floor vibrate. A rumble accompanied the feeling. Leanna rushed to the door and flung it open. Horses, maybe twenty-five of them. There were three riders. Each tipped his hat, acknowledging her presence. Glory be, what a wild beginning.

At the same time she heard a vehicle skid to a stop in the gravel parking area above the cabin. There, in her vision, stood Sam. His walk and size reminded her of John Wayne. He was hurrying toward her.

"Did you see those horses? I've never seen anything like that."

"The wranglers are taking them to the pasture for the night. The process will reverse in the morning."

"What time?"

"Possibly just before dawn."

"I'll be waiting."

Sam thought her excitement was like that of a fledgling. They stood side by side on the little porch watching the horses run. Her delight in something he observed every day penetrated his being. He felt a renewal of life itself. He almost turned and took her in his arms.

Instead, he took both of her hands in his and seated her in one of the chairs; then he took a seat in the other.

"We abandoned you earlier. I'm sure the kids went to the barns to let Dancer out. I had some urgent phone calls to make. Then it dawned on me what we had done. It was so thoughtless."

"I must admit, at first I was . . . uncomfortable. Then my brain kicked in, and I found it rewarding. I've been hiding under a bushel basket. It's time to jump out and say, 'Boo, guess who?'"

Leanna didn't know that Sam wanted to be there to watch and share that time with her.

"As a form of apology I've come to give you a lift. Usually you'll have to walk that third of a mile to the center of things on your own. I chose this cabin for you and Cindy because of the view."

"Are jeans the normal attire? I'd like to change."

"That's fine. I'll wait here on the porch." Sam would never tell her about the cancellations and changes of scheduling he'd just accomplished. "Poor Mom" was entirely different from what he had imagined. He never had a clear picture of the person he expected to get off the train. As an escape route he had set up a lot of business meetings and appointments for himself. Now he wanted to be free to enjoy Leanna's company and be part of most of the festivities. There were a few longstanding arrangements that would have to be honored.

As Leanna rummaged through the cases looking for her casual clothes she thought of Sam. No wonder Cindy spoke so highly of him. There was nothing outstanding about his countenance, but he radiated kindness, helpfulness, and generosity. She had also noticed that his brown eyes matched his son's.

She then thought of the money being spent on these few days; also the money the ranch was losing because of the arrangements. She made a promise to herself that this day must not end without a satisfactory solution.

Not to put off the confrontation, as she climbed into the van, Leanna spoke up. "I'm afraid I cannot start on my new plan until we straighten out one problem. The financial arrangement for all of this is off balance." She raised her eyebrows and looked over the top of her glasses. "I had forgotten that I was mad at you."

"I wish you had completely forgotten. Let's, you and I, go into town and eat supper. I'd very much like to put this to rest before a new day begins."

Sam stopped at the office and front desk to account for their whereabouts. Leanna walked through the dining area, which she found pleasing. If she had expected manicured grounds, chandeliers in a plush lobby, uniformed men to help with her bags her disappointment would have been overwhelming. As it was, she was as happy as could be. These people were real. Their acceptance was customary.

Leanna was thinking about Millie as they rode into town. The relationship that had developed between her and Cindy was obvious. Well, it would be a blessing for her daughter to have a Texas mother also.

Sam said, "Let's eat first. Then we'll get down to business."

Leanna waited patiently. As she popped the last bite of ham steak into her mouth and finished her iced tea, Sam requested a pot of coffee. Then he sat back. "Now plead your case. Let's put all disagreements on the table in plain view. We'll then rearrange them until there is no more thought of misbehavior. I am prepared to hear you out."

"Hear me out you will. A traditional wedding is to be covered by the bride's family. The groom's family pays for the rehearsal dinner.

"I can't even imagine what all of this is costing you. I could never pay for such goings on."

Leanna kept hesitating, waiting for his response. Sam would just motion for her to continue. It was clear that he would make no comment until her complaints were aired.

Leanna had a big list of thoughts, but at this moment the list had slipped from her grasp. She looked helpless. "Now that I have your full attention, I can't remember what I wanted to say."

"In the first place, this is not a traditional wedding. It's my son and your daughter." Sam continued, "We have the facility to provide these arrangements. Yes, some money is involved. I am fortunate enough to have been born into a family that has worked hard to get where we are today. What we have left of our family is extremely happy about this upcoming marriage. We all want to see Jimmy happily married and settled. When he brought Cindy home with him at Thanksgiving he spread a good feeling to everyone who lives and works on the ranch. We all love her like one of our own.

"She was a hard sell, too. She didn't think you'd agree to it. I don't know what changed her mind.

"She's worked hard on this, and, yes, so have I. We all have. We don't want any hard feelings. Usually when I work on a project, I never worry because, things are planned so carefully. I've discovered weddings and accessories are a headache. We've put all our effort into these preparations. Hopefully, there will be few difficulties.

"You have paid for one round-trip train fare, and a one-way ticket. A wedding dress and the many extras that go with it. Your own outfit. Plus, a lot of things I can't account for." Sam looked exasperated. "Shoot, now I've lost my list, too. You make me tongue tied as a schoolboy."

Leanna burst out laughing. "I rather doubt that. If I was a judge I'd wrap my gavel and declare you not guilty."

"If you still have funds that were set aside for this purpose we'll switch roles here and you can pay for the rehearsal dinner. Then if there's still change jangling in the bottom of your purse give it to the kids as a grubstake. They are starting out on little and both have refused help from me."

"Sold."

"Will you shake on it, and not another word about this money thing?"

"Done."

"You see, Leanna, you have forgotten something. You have put in twenty-some years. Years that were filled with love and the proper bringing up of a fine young woman. No one could have done a better job. You should be very proud. To me that's a lot more important than anything else."

"Goodness me. Have you ever lost a fight Sam?"

He sat a minute. When he looked at Leanna again there were tears in his eyes. "Yes, I lost one. I played every hand I had but I couldn't win; I lost my partner."

Leanna hung her head in remorse.

Sam stood and reached in his back pocket for money to pay the bill.

As they neared the van each had regained their composure. Sam held the door for her. "You're a lot prettier when you smile."

As he settled in the driver's seat Leanna said, "You, my friend, are a hard man to deal with."

Sam was passing the ranch house when she spoke again. "Let me out here please. I need that third of a mile walk tonight. That may be the most valuable part of my time here. It will allow me time to myself, to think, and to find out more about me."

As Leanna closed the door Sam called out, "See you tomorrow, friend."

Leanna smiled, then turned and started up the hill.

 CHAPTER 12

Leanna, half-awake, turned toward the clock she had placed on the stand between the beds. It was 5:30, and still dark.

All of a sudden, she remembered the horses. She scrambled out of bed trying not to waken Cindy. When she came out of the bathroom she was showered and fully dressed.

Leanna stepped out on the porch, with a sweatshirt tied across her shoulders. Hearing horses' hooves moving down the hill toward the pasture assured her that she hadn't missed the spectacle.

Daylight was just beginning to top the ridge when she heard them approaching. She remained seated on the steps, in full satisfaction.

One of the riders cut away and came toward her.

"Ma'am, how about a lift to the nearest coffee pot?"

"Sam, is that you?"

"That it is, and I never accost ladies when it's dark. Care to climb aboard?"

"I don't see a rumble seat. How would it be if I walked along side? Or better yet, met you there."

"You get in the saddle and I'll walk."

"I know nothing about horses and I hate to start my learning when it's still on the dark side of the morning."

Before Leanna could utter another word of protest Sam was standing beside her.

"You're not talking your way out of early morning coffee with me." The horse trailed along behind.

"I can't believe that you are normally part of this detail."

"Haven't done it in years. I wanted to check, firsthand, to see if you would really be up and watching for the horses. Breakfast isn't until 8:00 but we'll have a mug of coffee with the boys. I'll introduce you."

First off, Leanna noticed the big wide-brimmed black, sort of floppy hats. Obviously, they shielded the wearers' faces from the sun. As the wranglers hung them on the rack, each unveiled an extremely white forehead in comparison to the rest of his face. She was told that the work hats were made of wool, and that was why they were soft and pliable.

The last man in had a big feather stuck in the band of his hat. It reminded Leanna of when she had taken a trip to Natchez, Mississippi, and she had heard the historical story about the river men who landed "Under the Hill." Only one man would wear a feather in his hat, and he was considered "Cock of the Walk." The honor was hard fought, and was won only by the strongest. This tall, slender cowboy did not look like a brawler. Someone told Leanna that he was the one on the ranch who broke the horses. So, his looks were deceiving.

Cindy was in the dining area by 8:15. She and Leanna discussed their unpacking. They'd see what needed pressing. Sometime during the week Cindy wanted to show her mom the school, the little rented house, and the many things that would be part of her new life. How they would work it all in would be the problem.

"But first and most important, Mom, you have to meet Dancer." A quick trip to the barn revealed a dog full of energy and plenty of love to share.

Nothing like lots of wet and sloppy kisses right after breakfast. Leanna's reaction was just what Cindy knew it would be: love at first sight.

They had almost finished storing things in the chest of drawers and deciding what else needed doing when a voice was heard.

It was Jimmy. "Hey, Cin, why don't you finish up the work and let your mom go with me? The ranch bought a new horse in the next county. How about it, Leanna? You could ride along while I pick it up, and we could stop at the county seat and have a bite of lunch at the place where we're having the rehearsal dinner."

Leanna was delighted with the prospect. She had spent little time with her son-in-law to be. Cindy placed her hands on her hips. "Well, I suppose. Get going you two."

Leanna was a bit frightened when they loaded the horse. It was not cooperative, and Leanna, being unused to the routine, was feeling a mite shy. Staying out of the way seemed the safest thing to do. But they involved her in the process and she soon forgot her fear because she was too busy to concentrate on any negativity.

Lunch was grand. No wonder her daughter loved this young man. He was a joy to be with.

Every time Leanna went through the town nearest the ranch she wondered if it had shrunk. According to the sign the population was 1,000. It contained a post office, bank, gas station, a few small shops and restaurants. Not much.

While they were unloading the horse, Leanna caught sight of someone coming across the land at top speed. "Who's coming in the cloud of dust?"

Jimmy looked up. "Probably Taylor." With that he returned to his work.

The horse was pulled to a stop just feet from Leanna. "Are you Cindy's mom?"

"Yes, I am."

The girl vaulted from the horse and hugged Leanna. Leanna was flabbergasted. Even Jimmy stopped what he was doing and stared.

"If you're Cindy's mom, you must be a nice lady. I'm pleased to meet ya. Where is she? I need to tell her something."

Jimmy spoke up, "Cabin #28, I imagine." Horse and rider tore up the hill.

Leanna looked at Jimmy. He shrugged his shoulders. "Never seen her act like that before. Looks like you've got a friend."

Leanna finally found her voice. "I hope I don't disappoint her. By her actions I'd say she needs a friendship in return."

"Taylor needs a mother." Jimmy looked at Leanna with a solemn face. "Could you be a surrogate mother? I'd be beholden to ya."

Leanna was puzzled.

When he turned back to her he confessed, "I can't even explain that request to you. Let's just see what develops. Just be yourself. That's enough. But, be careful," he warned.

Leanna was even more puzzled.

She turned and headed toward cabin #28. Taylor's horse was cooling itself under a tree with its reins trailing on the ground. The door burst open and both girls stood in the doorway. "Well, Mom, guess you've met our Taylor." Taylor's face was flushed with embarrassment. Leanna put her arms around both of the girls' waists and the three of them entered the door laughing.

 CHAPTER 13

Saturday morning, July 5th. Now the crazies would begin. Guests would start arriving. Checking them in and settling them would be up to the staff. However, Leanna felt she should be somewhat available as a welcoming committee. At the same time the rodeo competitors were rolling in with pick-up trucks and horse trailers. The annual event was obviously a jubilant occasion.

Leanna sat down on a bench by one of the barns. A few quiet minutes would prepare her for the onslaught. She overheard Buc talking to a new young employee.

"It may look like a glamorous job, but believe me, it isn't. You not only work with the horses, you'll help with the calves. You'll build fences, pull windmills; whatever needs doing. If I see you sitting around, you're finished, on the spot. You never ask what to do. If you have to do that, we don't need you here. That's what your eyes are for. Wages are important, but cowboys do this kind of work because that is what they want to do. You understand?

"There's a one-week trial period. If we like your work and you still like it here, then we'll talk long-range employment. You still interested?"

"Yes, sir."

Leanna moved away before the young man came out of the door. She didn't want him to know anyone had been listening.

By 2:00 her good intentions were forgotten because the rodeo had officially started. Sam took her up to the announcer's booth. Over the noise he tried to explain the rules. Leanna could feel his closeness. She scrutinized him as he talked. She was impressed with him, and not strictly in the sense that she should be. She must quell these feelings. He was only being kind because she was Cindy's mother. She had not had feelings like this in so long she didn't know how to deal with them properly. Feelings like this were out of place here.

She moved her gaze down to the chutes and spotted Buc. He was explaining something to the young man by his side. Then he moved away. He could watch the kid but not be seen. In minutes the young fella was covered with dust and barely recognizable. Buc smiled and walked further on to speak to some of the wranglers. Growing up was fast in Texas, and it was not a choice. If you wanted a man's job you had to be a man. Leanna looked back at Sam and listened to what he was saying. Thank goodness the previous thoughts had vanished and she could concentrate on the rodeo.

The rodeo was for fun. It was a family outing. Lots of youngsters competed.

The loud speaker blared out, "Gentlemen: Oops, ladies also. This competition is not for money. It's for spirit. Let's see it, and hear it. Come on now. A big whoopla for the whole shebang." With that the volume of cheering tripled. The crowd went wild.

A few young men picked easy events so they could show off in front of their girlfriends. Also, the ranch hands, who normally didn't rodeo, were prodded into boisterous competition.

Later the voice on the speaker announced, "The competitors and their families share their potluck at the tables set up on the grassy area. The wedding guests and ranch hands head for the dining hall. If you are part of both groups, well, eat up."

Soon after the supper hour the neighboring folks left, and it became quiet.

The visitors had received some information papers that had been run through the copier in the office.

At breakfast Sam stood, welcoming everyone, and made some announcements of coming activities and whom they should see if they needed additional help. The only fact that drew a good-natured moan from the crowd was that the horses had Sunday off.

The family would leave for church at 9:30. Cindy was anxious for her mom to meet the minister who would be performing the ceremony.

Leanna thought he must have been hired from a movie studio, he was so perfect. He looked like Friar Tuck, who kept turning up in Sherwood Forest. The man seemed happy with life itself.

A cheerful smile should have covered up the devilish twinkle in his eyes, but it did not. What amusing secrets were being detained in his brain?

He was the Methodist minister for several small churches in the area. Still, he seemed to have plenty of time to listen to each person who requested a word with him. Leanna found him to be a delightful individual.

She could easily picture a person walking down a country lane with him, confiding any troubles. As she observed the faces around her, she had the feeling that many others had imagined the same picture.

 CHAPTER 14

Monday, July 7

It was 6:30 and they were all gathered at Millie's oilcloth-covered table. Sam informed Leanna that it was Gramps who hooked people up with a suitable horse. Following the second cup of coffee she and Gramps headed toward the barns.

"How's your horse sense, Leanna?"

"Awful, but the desire to learn is there."

"Then we've nothing to worry about."

Gramps brought out a gentle white horse and taught Leanna the proper beginning of horse care and safety. After mounting, Leanna exclaimed, "This is great!"

Gramps spoke up immediately, "Never get overconfident or cocky. Never."

Wiping the smile from her face, Leanna gave her full attention to the paces Gramps was putting her through.

Walking back toward the house Leanna said, "I know I've got lots to learn, but I still say it's great."

The program, to be given by a real cowboy, began at 1:00. As they neared the meeting room they could hear him singing and playing his guitar. Cindy and Leanna wouldn't have missed it. Listening to his speaking voice was half the fun.

He talked of branding and branding procedures. Even how to change a brand. He assured them that there still were rustlers about. The price of leather was set by Reebok, Nike, and Adidas.

He began to draw lines on the blackboard. It reminded Leanna of the coaches on TV Saturdays, when they explained their football plays. It was patterns used to bring in the cattle. How to utilize your experienced cowboys and the ones who would learn as the years passed.

"We still herd cattle the old-fashioned way around here, and personally I think it's the only way to do it. Horses and men; no helicopters, or other motorized vehicles."

He spoke of the history of the cowboy, the use of spurs and chaps.

Everyone in the audience was sorry when he drew the program to a close. But he promised he'd be around all week if any of us wanted to ask questions.

After supper, in the cafeteria, Sam slipped away with Leanna. He was anxious to show her the territory. "Do you have any questions about the way we live out here? My answers will be honest and true, I promise."

"Well, I should hope so." They both laughed at his statement.

Tuesday, July 8

Everyone piled on the old yellow school bus heading for the cow dog demonstration.

They are officially called "Hanging Tree Cow Dogs."

1/8 Catahoula Leopard

1/8 Kelpe

1/4 Australian Shepherd

1/2 Border Collie

Are they cute, cuddly, pretty? No.

Are they smart, well trained, hard working, and fun to watch? You bet.

To show the visitors how the dogs work, the rancher had moved a few head of cattle out in the hills. When the dogs located them, they would bark to let the rancher know. Then they would proceed to bring them in.

You don't insult the dog by taking too many dogs nor people on horseback. The rancher must know his craft. It's done with hand signals.

The hardest part is to get the dog to stop. They love their work. The ranchers have to be careful how they paired them up.

The females have a tendency to want to be boss. Sometimes the stock is in a rocky area where horses can't roust them out. The cow dog is invaluable at this point.

Cindy and her Mom had a grand time. The demonstration was fun to watch, and mingling with the guests added to the jollity. Their appreciation for these new things they were learning was obvious.

They were sitting around the table for lunch when Leanna asked, "Do you have someone coming to do pictures the day of the wedding? I haven't heard you mention a name."

"Oh, sure, I'm all set."

All faces turned toward Cindy and a chorus of voices asked, "Who?"

Cindy laughingly said, "Welcome to the owl family luncheon." She continued to eat just to stretch out the suspense. "I've asked Conner O'Malley to do them."

The Texas part of the family retorted, "Conner O'Malley! He's going into his senior year in high school. His expertise is wildlife photos. When did you meet him?"

Cindy loved the looks of disbelief. "I met him in April, the day I signed my contract. We've been in touch. I know his father owns the local hotel and his mom runs the restaurant. He has won some awards for his photography. He has a small darkroom off of a little workshop, off of his bedroom. It's in the back on the second floor. How about that?

"Besides I figured he'd be just the man for the job. Before the day is over I think a man with wildlife experience will be just what we need. I have given him a long list of what I don't want. There will be no posed group pictures, before or after the ceremony." She gestured nonchalantly with her hand. "Just scatter and have a good time.

"That answers the question, doesn't it?" She looked at each face for approval. Everyone just smiled and shook their head. Saturday would be an interesting day, full of little surprises. "If you show confidence in someone they will show you confidence. Conner will do fine. End of the report. I'm off to see my good friend Dancer, she doesn't ask any questions."

Immediately after the supper hour Sam invited Leanna to go horseback riding with him.

"I'll go if you'll remember that I'm a greenhorn."

"I promise to be patient with you if that's what you're worried about. I won't ride off and leave you out in the hills. There's something I'd like you to see."

They rode slowly away from the ranch, climbing higher. Leanna tried to relax as much as possible, so that Sam would not find riding with her tedious. She was relieved that he seemed comfortable with the slow pace.

The beginning of darkness was making her nervous. It was then that Sam said, "We must start back."

As they turned their horses around Leanna gasped. "This is what you wanted me to see, isn't it?"

Sam smiled. "I thought you'd like it. I've always thought it was a beautiful sight. Almost like a gift."

The ranch lights were coming on one by one. It looked like a small village.

"Thank you for sharing this with me, Sam. It is beautiful. It's no wonder you are so proud of the place."

They picked up their pace enough to get back before it was too dark. Brushing the horses down in their stalls they said little.

"May I walk you back to the cabin?"

"That would be a nice ending to an eventful day."

Wednesday, July 9

Cindy and Leanna went for a quick morning ride. The cool air on their cheeks felt good.

After cooling down the horses and cleaning themselves up in the cabin, they headed for town.

The rental house was a disaster. Cindy had been forewarned by Millie that all Jimmy had done was sleep there. It looked like someone had broken into an empty place and was using it strictly for a roof over his head.

"I guess my first project is this mess I'm standing in. At the same time I have a school room to prepare. There goes August."

"Good grief, we'll have to sleep in the car the night we get back from our honeymoon unless someone gives us sheets and blankets for a wedding gift."

"It seems unkind to barge in here now. Almost like I don't have the right to do so. Am I being odd, feeling that way?"

"Maybe, but I understand. Suppose I was to give you money for sheets, pillowcases, a bedspread, curtains, a couple of throw rugs?"

"It isn't so much the money as the lack of time. But I might just accept. It would be a nice gesture, and it sure would perk things up a bit. But I still wouldn't feel like it was right for me to come in here until we get back. Poor Jimmy would probably feel like he should sleep on the floor. One thing I've got to remember, it's not me anymore but we."

"Millie said she offered to come and clean up a bit and Jimmy acted like he was offended, almost hurt. Said something to the effect that it was our place, we'd do it. I better leave well enough alone."

They drove on to the school; as they went through the front door they met one of the other teachers.

After introductions the teacher called out, as she backed out the door with her arms full of books, "You're lucky to have someone helping you clean."

Cindy took it for granted the teacher was thinking her mother was there to work. The surprise came when they walked into her classroom to discover a man washing the windows. When he turned and tipped his cap she laughed out loud. "Conner, what are you doing?"

"Just helping out, ma'am." She went through introductions again. Shaking her head she showed her mother the room and explained some of her ideas for the class. When she turned again Conner had disappeared.

Leanna said, "Rather an odd fellow."

"No, he's doing just what I asked him to do. It's our secret."

As they left the building a car honked, and Cindy waved. "That was Jeremy Jones. He's a part-time wrangler on a nearby ranch. In his spare time he's a reserve cop and belongs to the county posse.

"I have a notion that he has had a crush on Taylor for a long spell, but he makes no move to let her know. She's so hung up on Parker Bates, she's probably never noticed Jeremy. It's a rotten shame. She'd be a lot better off. Jeremy is a nice kid. He and Jimmy are good friends."

That evening Sam asked Leanna to take a short ride. "You know, Sam, I'm getting quite comfortable with this horse stuff."

"That's the only way you learn. I'm glad you're enjoying it."

There were a group of the guests gathered in the dining area, so they stopped off to join them.

Leanna walked up to #28 with old friends who were housed in a nearby cabin.

Thursday, July 10

10:00. Big John the lion hunter.

Cindy wanted Leanna to meet Big John. She knew when writing home she would speak of the couple often. Accomplishing that, the two of them settled in for an interesting session. Cindy was to realize that there was a lot more to the man that what she had so far learned.

John spoke of bird banding and how the area was on the main flyway for the hummingbirds' southern migration in the fall. Then he got into his favorite subject: dogs and their training. Cindy could still picture them when she and Jimmy had gone calling. They were sad-looking dogs with loppy ears. But as John's story unfolded, Cindy's perception changed.

"If the state you are in has a hunting season for lions, a license is required. In Texas you do need a license, but there is no limit to the kill.

"If a Texas rancher is losing livestock because of a lion, I get a call from the rancher and do not need to contact any further authority.

"I carry a .38 caliber pistol or small carbine rifle. After the animal is destroyed I skin it and take the skull. Schools and other organizations can often use them as educational tools. The meat is edible. It's white meat with no gamey taste.

"A few years back we moved a lion out of Big Bend National Park to Florida. You use a dart, a cage, and then transport. Most of the time the lion will return to its home territory." He shrugged with that remark.

"I usually take one or two hunters and one student; five or six dogs, one young one for training.

"Most problems come in the spring because of calving, foaling, and baby kids dropping. Last year one female that weighed 134 pounds killed a hundred and nineteen goats in one night."

He had the group mesmerized.

It was at this point that he pulled out, leaving the audience behind. Cindy could see what was happening. John was heading further into the Davis Mountains. Not wanting to be left behind in this room, she closed her eyes and went with him. Leanna glanced at John and then Cindy. Then she, too, closed her eyes to follow.

"Sometimes we use horses or mules, other times it is too rough and you walk. In the summer it's best to leave around 3:00 a.m. to avoid the hot sun. I like to hunt at night but the terrain is rough on the inexperienced.

"Lions are territorial. The female has a range of 25 square miles, the male 100 square miles. This brings the female through the same territory every two to three weeks. The male will come through every couple of months looking for his females.

"Each lion has an identifying way of killing and eating its prey. It's exciting to watch the dogs work. Trailing a lion you discover how it moved the night before; under ledges, was it hurt, how far it traveled.

"The mountain lion is a predator and is probably not thinking that the dogs are trailing him. Sometimes they will get way up on a rock to fight the dogs. Usually they climb a tree thinking they can hide and escape. Never run. Then they will attack because of instinct.

"Once the dogs jump the lion he can only run 200 yards. It can be dangerous. Once my dogs were getting torn up. I had to get in the middle of the fight to stop it. You see, the dogs are part of our family."

It became quiet. Cindy shook her head as if coming out of a deep sleep.

"Any questions?" Leanna timidly raised her hand, and John nodded toward her.

"I'd like to ask a personal question. How do you feel when the job is completed? When you put your dogs in the truck and head home. Do you feel manly, exhilarated, sad; what?"

There was a pause.

"Pride, I feel pride. I'm proud of the dogs. I have taken them from a tiny pup to a three- or four-year-old, well-trained lion dog. Maybe I feel like a parent, or a teacher. And they then rest. I believe they know when it was a good job well done."

Simultaneously, the crowd rose to applaud. Many hurried up to talk to John further.

As they left, out the back door, Leanna took Cindy's arm. "Its people and land are fascinating. Such a privilege to learn about it firsthand.

"When Sam suggested these talks to entertain the guests, I had no idea it would be like this. The wedding may soon be forgotten but the events leading up to it will not. I'm so glad the guests brought their children. I have learned a great deal myself."

After freshening up, Leanna and Cindy walked down for lunch.

"Have you been able to spend much time with Jimmy?"

"He's working hard, and since he can do any job on the place, I'm never sure where he'll be. There must be a magnetic force between us, because each time I go directly to where he's working.

"Tuesday I just wanted to see him. Automatically, I went to the barn and saddled up. We met halfway up in the hills. He was coming to look for me." Nothing more needed to be said.

At the table Sam looked around at everyone but especially Leanna. "If there is anything you want to do, don't hesitate to ask. I'll try to arrange it."

Leanna spoke up. "Almost every morning and evening I have watched the wranglers move the horses to and from the pasture. Could I go with them sometime?"

Sam was on his feet immediately and took her arm. "Let's ask the boys."

One young man spoke right up. "No problem. We'll go about 4:00 this afternoon. We'll wait for you."

"You won't have to wait. I'll be there."

All afternoon Leanna hoped she looked relaxed and normal when she spoke to people. Inside, she was so excited she felt like she might be visibly shaking. Her heart was skipping with anticipation.

Even though it was early still, she walked to the small gazebo where you could watch riders mount up. Two of the wranglers' wives were resting there. Listening to them she discovered just how different their lifestyles were. Finally, she shared her excitement about the privilege she was being offered.

"So, you're going to jingle."

"What?"

"That's what they call it in this part of the country when the wranglers move the horses back and forth to pasture."

Leanna moved over by the gate just in time to overhear a voice say, "Don't forget to saddle an extra horse for the lady." The voices from inside the barn went silent.

Then the young man Sam had talked to at lunch came to her and sheepishly said, "I'm sorry, ma'am, but the boss said we can't let you go with us."

"Thanks anyway. I was surprised that you said I could go; insurances and all." Leanna headed back toward the cabin to change out of her jeans and worn shirt. She had waited there quite a while. Why hadn't they told her earlier? Was she experiencing disappointment, anger, or embarrassment? Most likely all three.

How deep was Sam's sincerity? Did he know how to keep his guests happy, then let the underlings do the underhanded work? Maybe his rules for honesty were for others.

Who had squelched the deal? She thought Sam was the boss. Not a soul mentioned the incident. It seemed odd to Leanna.

After supper Leanna pleaded exhaustion and headed slowly for the cabin. When passing the corral she leaned against the fence with her arms resting across the top rail.

She was concentrating on the horses and letting her mind wander. She heard a truck pass behind her, at slow speed, but was so lost in thought that she didn't hear it pull to a stop. She was startled when one of the men moved up to stand beside her.

"You like the horses?"

"Yes, I do. Maybe not a good thing for a city girl." Then he got back in the truck and drove slowly on down the road.

Just his stopping picked up her spirits a little.

Up the path further she ran into one of the other men. "Gosh, where did you get the big red scratch across your cheek?"

"There was a group of boys here just for the day. When we were driving the horses to pasture four of them came running toward the horses waving their arms and yelling. I wasn't half as mad at them as I was the parents. They thought it was a lark. They were up on the hill using their camcorders to record the scene.

"Twelve hundred pounds, twenty horses, coming at them full speed. What were those parents thinking of? We spurred our horses and were trying to avoid a horrible accident. Luckily we got them under control. A tree branch caught my face. Thank goodness it wasn't closer to my eye.

"One of us could have been hurt badly, or even one of the horses. I don't want to think what could have happened to the boys. The parents undoubtedly would have put the blame on the ranch.

"I rode back to make sure none of them was hurt. The parents were all smiling and said they were having a wonderful time. I'm so glad we were able to entertain them. I doubt if they even realized how close they were to a disaster."

Leanna was glad to get to the tranquility of cabin #28. She sat on the porch thinking. Well, Leanna, that's why only experienced riders jingle. Someone like her would have only added to the problem. Even though it was early, she fell asleep the minute her head rested on the pillow.

Friday, July 11

Cindy and Leanna left after breakfast for their last ride. They had just come up over a hill when Cindy caught a flash of something. She hurriedly looked around and saw a horse tied over by some bushes. Then she picked up the flash again. It was coming from a nearby tree. In the pit of her stomach she felt panic. Then it dawned on her who the intruder was. She thought, Well, let's make this an action shot.

"Mom, let's gallop toward the tree." They both took off, pulling up by some boulders just short of the tree. They were both tired and laughing.

After Leanna caught her breath, she asked, "Who do you suppose the horse belongs to?"

"Probably a cowhand using the bushes as an outdoor facility. We ought to get back." As they urged the horses into a fast trot Cindy gave a backward wave with her right hand. How did Conner know this was her favorite way to ride, and that she and her mom would be coming today?

The afternoon was deliberately restful. The rehearsal and dinner went as planned.

 CHAPTER 15

At 6:00 Saturday morning the three bridesmaids joined Cindy and Leanna in cabin #28 for doughnuts and juice. Then they were off to the church. When they were satisfied with the results they headed for Cindy's surprise at the motel.

They each had a bubble bath. Cindy was last; when she reentered the room she found everyone eating a fresh fruit cup and a muffin.

Cindy exclaimed, "What's this?" The girls all talked at once.

"We were in the midst of getting fixed up when a knock came at the door."

"A male voice called out: Refreshments, courtesy of O'Malley's. Is everyone decent?"

"Conner only stayed a minute but he got pictures of us being made up." The girls giggled.

Cindy said, "You were all decent, weren't you?" Then they all giggled again.

"We've got to get a move on. I can't be late for my own wedding."

Minutes later Cindy walked up behind Taylor, who was staring at herself in the mirror. "What do you see, Taylor?"

"Who is it, Cindy?"

"It's you. Some of the beauty that has been hibernating down inside of you has been brought to the surface."

The wedding got underway right on schedule.

While Leanna was proceeding to the front, two people happened to look up at Sam. The expression on his face was surprising. Millie glanced across the church at LC, who was returning her look. Each registered disbelief.

After Taylor had made her way to the front of the church, Sam felt a nudge against his boot. Out of the corner of his mouth Jimmy whispered softly but clearly. "Dad, you're supposed to be watching for the bride. Close your jaw and quit goggling at her mother."

Jimmy had had one request: he wanted Cindy to wear her hair down on her shoulders. Because of that she had laid her hat aside at the last minute.

When she stood in front of him and handed him a flower from her basket Jimmy saw nothing but the girl before him. He smiled, shook his head slightly and whispered, "I love you."

Then it was over. Months of preparation, and Cindy could remember so little. She thought, Don't fail me, Conner.

They arrived at the ranch and were welcomed by an abundant array of food. Lots of the flowers had been brought out from the church and were not only in the dining room but also in the activity room next door, where the dance was to be held.

Cindy rushed back to get another look at the food. There was a Steamship Round: hot vegetables, mashed and scalloped potatoes. The rest of the buffet table was covered with salad dishes and Jell-O's. Plus there were rolls and breads, olives and pickles, and a huge round of cheese.

There was a white cake and chocolate, each filled with a pudding center. That was according to Cindy's preference. The ladies had even included carrot cake and banana cake, each with yummy-looking frosting. And, of course, ice cream. The wedding cake would remain on display for awhile.

Cindy couldn't help it; she clapped her hands, it looked so appetizing. She called out, "Wedding party first, the rest fall in."

Sam chuckled. He stood and automatically took over directing the flow so things would run smoothly.

There was no reception line, but as soon as Cindy and Jimmy had finished eating they moved from table to table conversing with each guest. When they thought they had completed the journey each checked the crowd carefully to make sure they had missed no one.

While they were eating, the music provided by a DJ was drifting into the dining room.

As people worked their way into the dance area, the lights were lowered a little. The sounds were lovely and danceable. At this point they went through the ritual of the right people in the wedding party dancing with the right people down the line.

Jimmy danced with Millie. Leanna danced with Gramps. He said he was waiting for the fast dancing later, then he'd dance with the bride.

The DJ played until the country band was ready to perform. He told them he'd stick around to fill in for breaks and also at the end while the cleanup crew worked. Jimmy knew the fellow wanted to dance with some of the pretty guests.

As usual, all the girls, and even older women, were eyeing Parker Bates. The funny thing was, time and again he headed toward Taylor, but he was always cut off at the pass. It looked almost as if it were a planned attack.

Leanna was talking to Buc when she noticed a shy girl nearby. "Hello, Buchanan."

"I do believe you are needed elsewhere, Buchanan."

As soon as the ceremony at the church had come to a close it had begun to rain, just as predicted. The covered side porch, just off the dance area, was full of open umbrellas.

Then it was hoedown time. Every wrangler in the place was dancing up a storm. Those polished cowboy boots didn't slow them down. All of the bridal party, especially Cindy and Leanna, were having a marvelous time. The building itself must have been rocking.

As the evening wore on, and the crowd thinned out, the music got slower. All of a sudden Leanna was spun around by two strong hands and found herself snugly held in Sam's arms. She laughed up at him.

"I have not been able to dance with you the whole evening, Leanna. That proper one at the beginning doesn't count. You are too popular."

"It's been a lot of fun. I can't remember having danced this much in my lifetime. All evening I have watched you. You were not a wallflower either. You look very handsome. It must be the snazzy suspenders."

With those words Sam whirled her graciously right out the side door. The music picked up, but Leanna seemed lost. "What is the step you're doing? I can't keep up."

Sam grinned. "I call it the Texas Tango. I do the two-step to everything. If the music speeds up I add a little jig step. You'll catch on." With that he grabbed an umbrella and they moved out into the rain.

The next number was slow and romantic. They danced a few steps, then Sam stood still. Looking steadily into Leanna's eyes he bent his head and kissed her. What totally surprised Leanna was that it was intentional and strong. What surprised her even more was her rapid response.

A figure was about to step out on the porch. When she caught sight of the couple kissing in the rain she quickly pulled back into the shadows. She did not move or make a sound. When she realized who it was, a smirk crossed her face. The tap-tapping of the rain on the tin roof of the porch covered any noise she made in her departure.

Sam held Leanna close and they finished the number. Then Leanna pulled back and slowly raised her head. Looking into Sam's eyes she said, "I think we should get back to the guests."

"You're probably right." He looked as though he was going to tip her chin up and kiss her again.

Leanna placed her hand gently on the front of his shirt. They turned and walked back through the porch; Sam replaced the umbrella.

As soon as she had reentered the dance area, Mrs. Taylor's eyes had begun darting around, finding the best tables to spread the gossip. The bride's mother and the groom's father were cavorting around outside in the rain.

People did not want to believe her, but they were aghast at the thought.

Sam and Leanna entered from the porch door and the lights picked up the rain speckles in her hair. He guided her to the ice water punch bowl with the lemon slices floating on top. Each was drinking refreshments when Leanna glanced up and saw Cindy across the dance floor with a dreadful look on her face.

Leanna turned and set her cup on the table. "Excuse me, Sam." And she headed around the edge of the crowd toward her daughter.

"Cindy, what is it?" Cindy turned and hurried into the ladies' room, so Leanna followed. "How could you, Mother?"

"What are you talking about?"

"Kissing Sam, falling all over him, out in the rain like a . . . a hussy. Those lovely shoes all wet. Are you trying to ruin the wedding?"

This was no time for lies, but what should she say? Obviously, someone had seen them. Leanna was not only shocked, she was angry with her daughter's reaction. It had been a harmless occurrence. She had the urge to fight back, to get nasty, to say or do something that in the long run would be a very hurtful move.

"Cindy, we have gotten along for twenty-five years now. Would I wait until your wedding day to hurt you? Think about it. Every girl wants her wedding day to be 'over the rainbow' perfect. Your day has been just that. The pressure is off, so relax; be yourself again."

In the middle of Leanna's little speech, the restroom door swung open and closed quickly, and Taylor slid the lock from inside.

"Cindy, she's right. The accusations came from my mother. She's a snit. Every day she gets more weasel-y. I caught up with her and told her I thought it was time she left, that she had done enough damage for one day."

"Remember the day I met you? I told you that I'd have to run interference for you one day. Well, this is the day. I had a feeling she would try to cause trouble."

There was a quiet knock on the door. "Just give us a minute, we're havin' a short meeting here."

With Taylor's comments Cindy took a deep breath. "I'm sorry. I guess the work on the wedding finally caught up with me. It was probably just an innocent happening. I'm glad it's all over and we can get down to being normal human beings. I've railed off at Jimmy a few times this week. I'm thankful he didn't decide I was too much to handle on a daily basis.

"We are going to fade away soon, no big exit. I love you both. Forgive me my faults. You're right, Mom. No way will we let anything come between us." She hugged them both and gave her mom an extra squeeze. "Wish me luck on my future as Mrs. James Pride." She unlocked the door and was gone.

As Leanna and Taylor stepped into the hall they saw no one waiting. Whoever it was must have found another restroom. They stood there in the cooler air.

Leanna said, "Do you suppose it's bad luck wishing a new bride good luck in the setting of a public restroom?"

"How was it anyway?"

"What?"

"The kiss, silly. If I liked older men I think Sam would fit the bill just fine." She grinned and winked at Leanna.

"Quincy Taylor, you need a good talking to."

"Let's do it now."

Taylor pulled Leanna out a back door. The rain had temporarily stopped, but it had settled the dust from the road.

Taylor's grin had vanished. In place of it was the look of a troubled young woman. "Leanna, why is it that I always pick guys like Parker Bates? I adore him; all he does is hurt me and make me miserable. I want to find someone nice, the way Cindy did. The girl you are looking at is not the real me."

"Quincy, you can be fired up by someone to an explosive point, but then the momentum stops. All that's left is a terrible emptiness.

"Parker Bates wears his sexuality like a bright suit of armor. He's irresistible. You ever looked in the jewelry store window? What catches your eye? The biggest, shiniest diamond. But when it comes to the nitty-gritty parts of life, it pales in a hurry.

"Love is different. These cowboys who walk around here, look at them. They look like a pretty dull bunch. Get them with their women and the fire lights up in their eyes, too."

"Who could love someone like me?" Taylor burst into tears. Leanna was speechless. She wrapped her arms around this lonely child and held her tight. Taylor collapsed against her. Leanna thought, Please, help me to say and do the right thing.

"Love surrounds you. Reach out and touch it gently and it will multiply."

Leanna looked up as she saw a movement by one of the nearby trucks.

Recognizing Jeremy, she motioned for him to come forward. When he was close to her she mouthed the words, "Take her home."

Jeremy hesitated only a second, then stepped close and very softly said, "Quincy, could I give you a lift home?" She looked up in surprise. He offered her his clean handkerchief. She wiped her cheeks. "I could sure use a lift. My time ran out and my pumpkin coach disappeared. I don't have to tell you, Jeremy, that I'm not the girl you're looking at. I'm just plain old me."

Leanna was pretty sure Jeremy liked Quincy either way. She had seen the adoration in his eyes as he watched her dance with everybody else. She thought they were both going to cry. Stepping through the doorway she left them together.

As she emerged from the restroom hallway Sam took hold of her arm. "That was a long time in the bathroom. Are you okay?"

"I'm fine. Thanks for being concerned."

"LC gave me the nod. The kids have left."

"I know. Will they be happy, Sam?"

"If the wishes in my heart have anything to do with it, they sure will. Everyone is leaving. May I drive you to the cabin? I know you must be as tired as I am." As she stepped out of the truck he said, "Be packed up in the morning. You'll be moving to the ranch house. We need that cabin."

 CHAPTER 16

Conner was home well before midnight; camera equipment was cleaned and stored away. Working at the hotel and restaurant didn't compare with the week he had just put in.

Surprisingly, he didn't lay awake with the many thoughts that were running into each other in his brain. Someone might have given him knockout drops, the way his body responded to his bed.

He had planned to rise early, but that didn't happen. Around 10:30, he woke and showered. He pulled on clean underwear, socks, and jeans and staggered down the stairs. Conner plopped in a kitchen chair and stared into space.

Both parents smiled. "So, the bride worked you pretty hard this week," and his father laughed. His mother said, "I'll fix you something to eat. It will give your body a wake-up call."

"Do you need me at the hotel or anything? I'd like to have these pictures ready when Jimmy and Cindy get back. I have to get the article ready for the paper at the county seat. There is a tremendous amount of work to do on the films. It's important to me to produce what she wants."

As his father walked from the room he said, "Still plenty of summer help around. You finish the job right." Before Conner left the kitchen he made his mother promise to call him if something needed doing.

His first job was to get everything organized. Moving into the darkroom he was nervous. The reason he was still tired was because of all the extras he had done. Now if his ideas would just pan out.

Conner had never been under pressure with his photography before. After the first six pictures had come through, he was flying high. By afternoon, he could have cried with joy. At one point, he nearly stumbled over the lunch his mother had brought up. He hadn't even heard her.

She called up the stairs for supper. Grabbing the untouched lunch tray, he headed down. "I'm sorry. Guess I skipped lunch." They could see he was more at ease. "It's going to work. My ideas are going to work."

Wolfing down his meal, he headed back upstairs. His excitement was mounting. Nothing could hold him back. He worked late and was up early. Some were just pictures, a record of an unforgettable occasion. Then there were the others that were exceptional.

It was quiet work. Oftentimes it was the interpretation and cross-maneuvering that took time. He wanted the best.

On the fourth day, his mother found him sound asleep in his easy chair. She gently shook him. "Come and have a good supper, son."

"Mom, this roast beef is the best ever."

"It's the same as always. You are letting your body taste food again. Got chocolate cake for dessert."

"Mom, Dad, I did it. I'm finished. I need to get it ready for presentation. I'll do that tonight. Would you like to have a look when they're ready?"

"Let your mom have a look-through. Lookin' through pictures is woman's doin's. I'm proud of you, taking on such a job. I'm sure they are good."

Before daybreak Conner was up. He sat with Cindy's two letters in his lap. How many times had he read them?

Conner,

More no's.

No drinking, smoking, champagne toast.

If that is a necessity for people, they will have to take care of it elsewhere, but not at my wedding. There will be hot coffee, ice tea, and Mom has a great recipe for orange punch. For dancing time—tubs of pop in ice, for the kids.

Pretzels, and some other snacks.

Punch bowls with ice water and lemon and lime slices.

Why am I telling you all of this? No cake cutting by the bride and groom. Those wonderful ladies in the kitchen will take care of that. No feeding the groom cake and smooshing it in his face. Special people I need pictures of:

My Mom	Millie and Fred
Jimmy's Dad	LC and Buc
Taylor, maid of honor	(Dancer and Blaze)

2 girls from Michigan, bridesmaids ETC.

No garter tossing to single men. No bouquet throwing to single girls.

I'm going to give it to Taylor, for luck.

We never talked about money. For years I've been saving pennies in a huge glass peanut butter jar. That should take care of it. I'm taking up so much of your time; it would be like calling a repairman. The expense is not so much what he does but getting him there, and his time. Not to worry. When we are finished I know it will be costly. I'm only planning on doing this once in a lifetime.

Thanks, Cindy

Conner,

No veils no lace.

No silverware pinging against water glasses until the bride and groom kiss. That's Jimmy's and my private affair.

I don't know the wedding traditions in your part of the country. Maybe some of the things I speak of startle you and sound out of place. Then again, maybe Texas does some things I disapprove of.

I kept quizzing Jimmy, but he'd just say, "Fine, whatever." Men are not helpful in these important matters, Conner. What's a girl to do?

Could you get some good shots of these events?

Thur. Train arrives.

Fri. Nothing

Sat. Rodeo

Sun. Church

Mon. Cowboy with guitar

Tues. Cow dog

Wed. Mom and I visit school

Thur. Big John

Fri. Nothing

Sat. Wedding — arrive early, you'll see why. Time schedule at ranch.

If you want to attempt a double exposure (or whatever you call it) with a few of your animals in the wild, in the background, give it a go. I can do no more than turn it down. Three cheers for imagination.

I love you for your patience. I know, to be proper, I should use the word appreciate in place of love. But it wouldn't say what I mean.

C. U. Soon,

Cin

He had scrawled May on one and June on the other. Her letters were a bit strange, but what surprised him was that he understood them. Maybe it shouldn't have surprised him at all.

It had all started back in mid-April. He had pulled his car over at his favorite spot for shooting. He always unloaded the camera equipment in that little turn-off, then made two trips back into the trees.

He heard another car door and looked up. She looked to be in her mid-twenties. He thought she probably wanted to ask directions. "Hi, can I help you there? Looks like you have too much for one load."

He paused a minute and then said, "I guess it would be a help." Who was she, he wondered? She was acting like this was a routine expedition.

Finally, he stopped. "Let's rest a minute, this stuff gets heavy."

She popped right up with, "What's your name?"

"Conner O'Malley."

"How did someone with a name like that end up in Texas?"

"It's complicated. My folks' last name is O'Malley. They moved here, had a baby boy, and liked the name Conner. What's your name?"

"Cindy Fillmore."

"Well, suppose I was to ask you a silly question like you asked me?

"Touché, Mr. O'Malley."

They laughed and leaned back against some tree trunks.

"Why did you stop to help me?"

Cindy shrugged her shoulders. "Looked like you needed it. Besides, I'm pretty wound up. I'm getting married in July and I just signed a teaching contract. It looked like a good way to bring myself back down to earth."

"This is one of my favorite spots. I go back here and get shots of some wildlife. Sometimes there isn't any. But it seems to be a well-traveled path for deer and smaller creatures, even birds. I've won some photo contests. Most of the time I spend waiting. Some of them seem like friends. It takes a while to get them used to my presence. When I reach a certain point on the trail, silence is the secret."

"You know what, I could use your talent. I haven't hired a photographer for the wedding yet."

"I've never done anything like that. Who are you marrying?"

"Jimmy Pride." She put on a happy face.

"You're the girl from Michigan? Well, I'm happy to make your acquaintance."

"Don't tell me with all this fancy stuff that you can't do a simple wedding." She sat still, scowling and thinking, for a minute. "No way, this is not going to be a simple wedding. This wedding is going to flip some lids."

By this time Cindy had Conner thinking.

"Listen to me. This is my, our wedding. There will never be another just like it." She proceeded to tell him details that she had shared with no one.

Cindy wrote her name, address, and phone number on a slip of paper she had in her purse, then took down the same information from Conner.

In standing, Conner said, "Could you keep your mouth shut long enough to sit a few minutes in my silent area?" She nodded yes with enthusiasm.

They sat side by side watching some rabbits when he saw her draw in her breath, and freeze. There they were, the pair of them. This seemed to be their favorite spot also. Another time, he hoped to tell her that hunting season had just finished and now the bucks would find their mates. He snapped the picture with his remote. The deer moved on, at a slow pace.

Cindy exhaled. On another piece of scratch paper she wrote: The wedding will be a . . . snap. I'm counting on you." She stood and brushed off the seat of her pants. Then she shocked Conner by giving him a quick kiss on the cheek, and she was gone.

He remembered wondering at the time if he'd been dreaming. Had she been real?

By this time, however, he knew the answer. He adored this woman. Hopefully, they would remain friends for a lifetime. She was eight years older than he, but a friendship like theirs crosses the age barrier. Their minds traveled the same paths. They would think of each other when their lives became tangled, and it would solidify their beliefs in human nature.

 CHAPTER 17

The morning after Cindy arrived, in July, Conner stopped by the ranch to finalize some details. They had gone into the dining area where it was cool and quiet. He checked out the lighting while she talked.

"Conner, I don't want to see one formal pose in those pictures. None of that time-consuming silly business. I want everyone to be relaxed and having a nice time. Casual poses, people mingling and acting natural; that's my fancy." She changed the subject. "Would you like me to see if I could find us a glass of lemonade in the refrigerator?"

He was going to respond, but realized her mind had already slid past the lemonade. She began to speak again.

"You see, Conner, as much as I like you, and you would add charm to any event, I want you to become invisible for a week. I want you to become so much a part of everything that no one notices you."

She stood and did a funny little dance. "Because of there being two different groups, folks will think you are a wedding guest. And you are, but a very special one. One who will see things through different eyes. I have a feeling that oftentimes you will see things as if through my eyes. Yes, I do."

Conner sat and folded his arms across his chest. "Do you talk all the time, girl?"

"Someday you will know me better, and you won't have to bother me with these questions. I'm just trying to cover a lot of information in a small amount of time."

"Did I tell you that sometimes I write for the paper? So, I can cover your wedding. That's one thing you don't have to think about."

"You are so talented that I may hire you as a companion. No, that's not a good idea."

Cindy walked back and forth among the tables. "Let's see, no 'dollar a dance' thing. If someone wants to dance with the bride of groom, all he or she has to do is ask. None of this cutting in. I don't like that.

"I'll not be ordering little books of these pictures to give to the parents at Christmas time. No big pictures for my house. None of that. I want lots of regular photos that I can look at on cold and rainy nights.

"The men of the groom's party are on their own. For the ladies I have something special planned. Women need to feel feminine for such an affair. Feel good, look good, I say. You'll see.

"I may not be able to talk to you again until I return from my honeymoon. Then we will sit and visit like real people." With those words, Cindy had blown Conner a kiss and had run out the door to catch up with someone else she wanted to talk to.

Was she scatterbrained? Not in the least. His mother had said Cindy would be tight as a fiddle string those last days. "A bride wants everything to go well. Cindy is crossing over and back on some traditions. She wants the transitions to be a success." His mother was a wise woman.

Conner had thought about possible ideas and plans after he had talked to Cindy that first time. He'd done a lot of scouting around, and background pictures were piling up. Then he moved into action. It became a game. People thought he was a guest from the other side of the family, or a friend from college. It was a challenge. It was also fun and informative.

The wedding day would not soon be forgotten.

Cindy's bridesmaids from Michigan had not only done the calligraphy for the formal invitation, but they also had worked with her on the first announcement that had been mailed. Plus, they knew how to work with hairstyles, facials, and makeup. Cindy had paid for their flight out and back.

Cindy's surprise was that arrangement had been made for two connecting rooms at the local motel the morning of the wedding.

Conner had discovered the early morning plans for the girls by accident. It provided him with twofold information. While he was eating breakfast that morning he watched a large florist delivery truck pull up and park by the church. Later he had taken telephoto shots of the girls going into the motel in jeans and T-shirts.

Conner had arrived at the church an hour and a half early. He let himself in a side entrance. Cindy had told him to come early. Thank goodness he had plenty of extra film in his car. If this was an indication of what was to come. . . . His thoughts had given way to the flash of his camera.

Cindy and the ladies had turned the plain little church into something spectacular. None of the usual white flowers that set the formal background. There was a variety of baskets, pots, crocks, and every imaginable container. Hothouse flowers and plants, greens; even some herbs. He got a whiff of spearmint.

There were more colors than were in a crayon box. The vivid colors, of every hue, had transformed the setting into a country garden.

Sunbeams streamed through the stained glass windows. Surprisingly, the room did not appear overdone. The flowers drew you in, as if to say, "Come join us on this special day."

Conner wondered if the ushers were going to slip allergy pills to those who might need them, so that the ceremony would not be broken up with sneezing.

Time had escaped him. The organist began to play some music softly. Conner took several pictures of local people as they were ushered in. The look of astonishment as they viewed the flower-laden church would delight Cindy.

Cindy had paid no attention to protocol. She was strong enough, inside, to say, This day is mine. No one contested her choices.

Jimmy and Sam, and the three ushers, came in the side door up by the front. They were dressed in light gray western-style tuxedos with boots and hats to match. They represented strength. They were Texans.

The guests waited.

When Leanna started down the aisle they knew the contrast of vision that they would behold. No frills on display here. On display would be the beauty of womanhood.

Leanna did not look younger than her years. Her hair was graying and worn short. Her dress had a high neck and sleeves; it was a soft pastel pink. Her makeup was subtle. Her only jewelry was a pearl necklace so simple it emphasized the elegance of her dress with its pearl buttons down the front. Her hat was the same pale shade of her dress with huge flowers. She carried a matching flower in her hands. When she looked at the flower her hat tilted down so you could only see the profile of her nose, lips, and chin.

At this point Conner recalled, Cindy had told him about the hats. She had a college friend who lived in New Orleans. She was a hatter and ran a boutique. Cindy had sent pictures of the girls and told about their personalities. She had included swatches of the dress material.

Leanna seated herself in the front pew.

Next came the two friends from Michigan.

When Quincy Taylor put her small foot across the doorstep Conner was amazed. He doubted if the locals recognized her. Where was the evidence of that wild tomboy?

Across the aisle, Jeremy Jones was leaning over the back of the pew in front of him to catch a glimpse of her. When he did see how she looked he nearly tumbled over onto a small child who had fallen asleep on the seat. His face turned crimson, but no one noticed.

She reminded Conner of Audrey Hepburn. Petite, feminine, delicate; she glided down the aisle. Her dress was a very pale blue; there were a few tiny pleats across the bodice. Her hair had been trimmed and styled. Her hat had a swatch of the same blue material as her dress in a pleated fan design and tiny soft white roses. Taylor looked like a living china doll.

She carried a small basket with white rose petals in it that she gently dropped along the way, as if to guide the coming bride to her destination. As she passed Parker Bates he reached out toward her. She moved smoothly away from him with no acknowledgment.

There was a slight silent pause.

The organist began to play a light rhythmic summertime medley. Down the center aisle came the bride. Her gown was white. The bodice was covered, front and back, with small pleats. The pearl necklace had belonged to her grandmother. The full-gored skirt proved luxurious-looking as she moved. Showing just above her shoes, with pleated buckles, were those shapely ankles.

Carrying a large basket of mixed colorful flowers she gaily strolled toward the altar. There was nothing solemn about her, and she never took her eyes off James.

When Cindy reached the front, she bowed slightly and handed him a flower from her basket.

The minister was about to bring some normalcy to the service; but he was interrupted. A hummingbird had been lured in through an open window by the flowers. It kept darting around the minister's head as if to convey an important message. Finally, the reverend looked at the bride and groom and said, "I believe our little friend is wishing you many years of happiness. It is a good omen."

He was about to begin but the hummingbird became confused. First, he darted to a flower and then tried to find the window where he had come in.

Looking on was like watching a rehearsed pantomime. Every head in the church was following the back-and-forth movement of the hummingbird.

Would it hit the window and fall? Would it turn into a bad omen instead? Finally, it found its escape route. There was a group sigh, and the wedding resumed.

From there on it was serious, traditional, and official. A happy occasion, indeed.

 CHAPTER 18

There had been no inkling of the move to the ranch house. But Leanna had everything packed in no time.

That Sunday morning she walked down to the dining area to visit with her friends over breakfast. When Sam came in he talked to everyone and wished them a safe trip home.

Before noon they had all cleared out, and Leanna's things were settled in a bedroom at the back of the house, where it was quiet. There was a bright and cheery guilt on the bed and pillow shams to match. It had to be Millie's handiwork.

The balance of the day was left open for everyone to relax. The food was light and easy, leftovers, and fix-it-yourself style.

Everyone disappeared mid-afternoon. Leanna imagined that they were catching a nap. When she stretched and yawned and looked at the clock on the antique night stand, she was embarrassed to see that the afternoon had dwindled away.

Freshening up she went downstairs; locating everyone by hearing ice cubes tinkling as lemonade was being poured into large glasses.

"What a beautiful pitcher. Is it a family heirloom?"

Sam answered. "Well, good morning, Glory. Yes, it is, goes way back but no one seems to know the history that goes with it. Sit and I'll pour you a glass. We are resting up because tomorrow this place will be buzzing again." Everyone nodded in agreement.

Buzzing it was. Even when Leanna woke early in the morning the atmosphere was different. She dressed in a flash and went down to see if she could help with anything. Millie sent her over to the cafeteria for breakfast. As soon as she returned she walked into the kitchen.

"Let me do something." Before anyone could utter a word she felt a hand on her elbow.

"You come with me. Everything is covered here. You and I are going riding to get away from the hubbub." Sam had already saddled the horses. It did seem good to get away from the confusion.

They stopped at the top of a hill. Leanna closed her eyes and breathed deeply. She opened them to look over the expanse of land. When her eyes reached Sam's, she discovered he was watching her intently.

"Wide open spaces. There's a wonderful freedom to it, isn't there, Sam?"

"If I had a camera I'd take your picture. It shows what this kind of land can do to a city person."

But to himself he thought, I don't need a photograph to remember you. Leanna had been in his thoughts more than he cared to admit.

They rode slowly up the mountain trails until it started to get hot, then headed back.

As they sat around after supper Sam explained to Leanna that he had an important meeting in Dallas that had been set up months ago. Quite a few ranchers were gathering to discuss business. Also to talk about the government's influence and involvement; and hopefully how to solve some serious problems that were affecting them all.

He would fly out of Midland before the sun was up. Hopefully he would make it back Wednesday afternoon. He excused himself so he could pack.

LC turned to Leanna. "Would you like to go for a long ride tomorrow?"

"Sure."

"I'm talking all day, hard riding. There's something I have to check on. We would have to leave before dawn. We'll be a long way from the ranch. You will see some beautiful country. We have to leave early to avoid the heat of the afternoon."

Leanna sat in deep thought, finally she looked at LC. "My mind says, how wonderful. What I question is my stamina. My ability can't compare with your experience. Can I make it? I refuse to be a hindrance."

"I would not have suggested it if I didn't think you could make it. But it will push you to the limit. We'll rest along the way. Best you retire early because I'll come by the house to pick you up at 5:00."

"So, you are offering me a challenge, and promising that you won't bring me home slung over the horses back like a dead carcass."

LC presented a crooked smile. "No guarantee, Ma'am."

"He's a scoundrel. What's your opinion, Millie?"

"I agree. But I'll have the food packed and ready."

Leanna asked, "Rain or shine?"

LC answered, "I'll take a slicker for you, but it is supposed to be clear tomorrow."

After LC had headed for his sleeping quarters, Tim spoke up, "My son Randy is going to compete in a rodeo in the next county the following evening. We have to leave mid-afternoon. Would you like to join us?"

"Do you think I will have recuperated by then? I'd love to go."

"You can let me know after lunch that day."

Sam had moved the truck up earlier. As he climbed in Leanna rose from her chair and stood on the steps of the house. He turned the key and gave a quick wave of his hand. She stood there waving until he was away from the house.

He almost circled around the drive and said to heck with the meeting, but he knew he couldn't. It was essential that he be there as representative of the ranchers in the district. It had been a long, long time since a woman had cared when he was leaving home. He forced his mind to concentrate on the seriousness of this meeting.

● ● ●

At ten minutes of 5 the next morning Leanna heard horses' hooves on the gravel outside. She jumped to her feet grabbing the lunch that Millie had packed in a special carrier. Giving her a quick hug, she said, "Wish me luck."

LC helped her into the saddle. As soon as they left the ranch yard they were encompassed in darkness. Leanna said, "I'm not complaining but I can't see a thing. Will my horse follow yours?" No answer. "Hello."

"I am here. Your horse knows what he is doing. It will lighten up soon. Can you see your horse?"

"No."

"But you can feel him. Watch where you think his ears are. When you begin to see them daylight won't be far behind."

A few minutes later she made another stab at conversation but received no response. She was relieved when the horse's ears appeared. The horses moved into a comfortable fast walk.

Coming to the top of a hill, LC stopped and motioned for her to do the same. He then moved ahead of her and turned his horse to face her. He touched his lips with his fingers for silence, then put his index finger to his ear; after that he pointed to his eyes and slowly closed them. She followed his example. The morning noises, or lack of them, were more pronounced. They sat this way for a few minutes. Then LC began to speak.

"Listen to my voice. Your endurance will be stretched. There will be times when you do not like me very much. Today is a learning day.

"As you sit with your eyes closed, remove your feet from the stirrups, relax your body; almost to the point where you feel like you could doze off in the saddle. Now settle your bottom down in the saddle, leaning back just a little. Shoulders back. Chin up.

"Normally, before mounting you would check your horse over. Ears, check for mites. Check his body for any injuries, or bumps. In the movies or on TV it looks like all you do is hop on and ride. Hop off and walk away. You have to take care of this horse. They act tough like they are in charge. In truth, they depend on you for care and guidance.

"You must be the one in charge, for the horse's sake and your own. Today we'll work them hard and long. Tonight we must reward them with extra care. The trick is to look after each other; mutual respect.

"Check your horse's eyes. Make sure they are clean. If a horse is scared his eyes will show it. If his ears are back, you better think quick; check around, something's wrong.

"Horses are skitterish. That's why it's important that you look around. You can see with more range than he can. If you see something up ahead that may frighten him, reassure him that everything is okay.

"There has to be a special bond for you to get the most from each other. If something startles either of you it's necessary for you to be prepared to react fast. You can be sure he will.

"We will start off with a very slow walk. Don't be frightened. I will ride next to you. If, for any reason, your horse should shy or make a quick move, I will have hold of your reins instantly; and have him under control.

"As your horse moves feel his muscles working. Let your body flow and glide with his. For today, you and your horse will become one."

Because of the complete concentration, Leanna began to feel the smooth mechanics of the moving horse. Being in such a relaxed state, her body began to sway slightly with the horse's forward progress.

"Put the toes of your shoes back in the stirrups, resting on the ball of your foot." A few minutes later he said, "Open your eyes. I sometimes think eyes and ears are not coordinated correctly.

"You must constantly be aware of what is going on around you. Even here, things appear peaceful, but there are wild animals. When seeing anything out of the ordinary you must let someone know as soon as possible."

Leanna was curious. Why this new ranch hand training? "May I ask a question?"

LC looked at her with a steady gaze. "Later."

And so the lesson continued. The sweat began to mark her shirt. Her hair felt like she had been driving cattle for days. Her skin was covered with the dry soil that they kicked up, because there was never enough rain. Her lips felt dry, but she didn't want to wet them with her tongue.

They pulled up to a watering hole and let the horses drink and graze. As they leaned against a tree for shade, LC smiled and made a comment, "I know how tired you must be. Go ahead and curl up and take a nap for a few minutes if you want." Making a pillow with her arm she dropped off instantly.

It was the knickering of the horses that woke her. "The horses say it's time to move on. Your question?"

"I was just wondering why? Why this compact individual class?"

"Each of us searches for contentment. We are not always aware of what we seek. And do not always recognize it when we come upon it."

He then turned away from her. "Mount up. There is still a long day ahead of us."

They stopped at lunchtime by a creek bed. A scattering of trees gave relief to horse and rider. The cold water felt good on her hands. Leanna thought of taking her shoes off but held back on that. The prepared lunch tasted like a banquet. They had removed the saddles to give the horses a deserved cooldown time.

"The rains are good this season. Some years the atmosphere is so dry it evaporates before hitting the ground. Other times it comes in torrents. Then it hits the ground so hard it doesn't have an opportunity to soak in. It fills the creeks to overflowing, and can cause some ranches to be cut off from the main roads.

"The lack of natural water is why most ranches have gone out of the cattle business. When the drought holds for several years it takes up to 90 acres to feed one steer.

"Instead, they go into the people business. I haven't decided which is easier to handle. They herd up about the same." He chuckled with that.

"Who do you suppose sets the market price for leather these days? The company that makes the sneakers you're wearing." And he again laughed. "Times have changed."

They saddled up again. Leanna began to realize just how exhausted she was. Spending the first part of the afternoon roaming this Davis Mountain area presented a serene picture.

At times, they rode side by side, traveling fast. They were dodging one way and another, making quick turns and doubling back. Trying tasks for a beginner. LC stopped abruptly and pointed ahead to the left. There were deer in a stand of trees.

As they observed the quiet scene the deer straightened, looked alarmed, and scattered. Leanna looked sideways at LC, who had stiffened in his saddle and was listening intently. Leanna was going to ask what was happening, but LC motioned for silence.

He then motioned for her to follow. They moved as quietly as possible near the top of a hill. Dismounting, they crept to some brush so they wouldn't be seen.

Leanna thought they were off of Pride land but wasn't sure. Below them, several men were moving a small herd of cattle toward some trucks.

JA crew waited there to load them. LC reached for a small tablet and pencil in his shirt pocket. "We need to ride hard and get back to the ranch as soon as possible. I have some calls to make. These boys will get away but the word needs to get out. They should be able to apprehend them somewhere along the line. Rustlers in the area can be a great loss. There are too many of them for me. I would never take a chance with you along. They think they can get away with it because it is in a remote area."

They ran back to the horses, trying not to frighten them with their speed. "Stay close to me Leanna and hang on." Two hours later they rode into the barn area with dust flying behind them.

The ranch hands recognized trouble. They reached for the bridles as soon as LC and Leanna brought the horses to a halt. LC jumped to the ground and headed for the barn office on a run. Leanna tumbled off the horse and into Buc'S arms. Rustlers was the only word she could get out. He set her on her feet and helped her to a nearby bench. "You get on up to the house, as soon as you can stand. Millie will see to you.

"You boys see that those horses are cooled down. Take good care of them. I'm in with LC and the phone. I doubt if there's anything to be done at this point but I'll check it out. Don't be alarmed but do be alert. There's been some funny stuff going on recently."

As he hustled along, he thought they had let a few happenings slip through their fingers because of all the celebration going on at the ranch. Carelessness was unforgivable. Perfect timing for a clever thief. Everyone within miles knew they would be concentrating elsewhere.

When Leanna got herself calmed, she proceeded slowly to the house. Millie took one look at her and hurried her upstairs and into a hot tub, getting the whole story in the process. "Gracious, you've had a full day and then some. Don't fall asleep in here. Don't need a drowning to end our day. Just put your sleepwear and robe on, come down; I'll have something for you to eat."

"I'm not hungry," Leanna managed in a shaky voice.

"You will eat something. Then I'm tucking you in. You'll probably sleep through 'til morning. Don't worry about it. Sleep as long as you can."

LC came in to check on her while she was eating. "First off," he said, "I've done all I can for now."

"You need something to eat LC?"

"I'll get a bite in the bunk area, thanks anyway. I'm too riled up to eat decent grub."

"You were right, LC. It was a beautiful remote area. Why does someone have to spoil it? I had been thinking that if all people had an opportunity to be out like that maybe there wouldn't be so much trouble. Then we ran into trouble itself. I am going to try and forget that part of our excursion. A day like this should be savored, pulled into your heart and tucked away. Drawn out . . . remembered when needed."

LC liked this woman. She belonged here.

• • •

Leanna slept until almost lunchtime. As she and Millie were eating a bite, Tim showed up. "Hear you had a rough day yesterday. Our rodeo invitation is still open. You up to it?"

"The desire is strong but I don't know about the rest of me."

Millie said, "You know, Fred and I were thinkin' of showin' up just in time for the rodeo itself. I know Leanna would be interested in all the preliminaries but that gives her another alternative if she's still pooped when you leave. If she can't take either, we'll leave her here to rest."

Leanna said, "Let's leave it open like that."

As soon as Tim went back to work Millie sent Leanna up for a nap. "I don't think I have any sleep left."

"You wanna bet."

Leanna did go with Millie and Fred; she fell sound asleep, leaning against Millie's shoulder, on the way home.

• • •

Sam walked into the house after everyone was in bed. The phone rang and he picked it up quickly so as to wake no one.

"Sam, it's Big John. Could I draw upon your time? We've got a mountain lion that's turned nasty. From all indications it's injured because of a scuffle with another animal. I need an additional man in order to feel good about the hunt, under the circumstances."

"I've been up to Dallas and just got home. Could you give me a couple of hours of sleep?"

"I could pick you up as late as 4:00. This one has been causing serious trouble close to your place. That's why I thought you'd have an interest."

"Count me in." Sam left a note on the kitchen table.

• • •

Tim stopped for just a second while Millie and Leanna were eating breakfast. "Tim, the rodeo was something else. Maybe sometime I'll be here visiting the kids, and I can join you, so I can see the program from your side of the fence."

"You promise?"

"Certainly, that will give me something to look forward to."

After helping with the dishes Leanna went upstairs to get her things packed up. The day passed slowly. Inactivity let her body start winding down. She had walked to the horse barn to spend some quiet time with Gramps. She'd surely miss the old gent. Just being near him had a calming effect.

In the late afternoon, Millie and Leanna were sitting on the porch peeling and slicing apples for pies, to help out the dining staff. Every once in a while Leanna would pause and let out a long sigh.

"Have you enjoyed your visit to the wild west?"

"Too much, I'm afraid. To be honest with you, I find it hard to leave. The trouble with such an experience is the knowledge that you must return to reality. It's real nice where I live, too. Maybe I shouldn't have gone along with Cindy's idea of an extended stay after the wedding. Everyone has been exceptionally kind."

"Plus, you have fallen in love with my brother."

The paring knife Leanna had been using slipped out of her hand and fell into the big pan of apples in her lap. She leaned back, closing her eyes. She appeared so distraught that Millie set her own apple pan on the floor and patted her hand.

"Don't worry, Leanna. I think I'm the only one who knows." And Millie's sigh matched Leanna's.

"Cabin #28 never was needed. . . . You know, I've never known LC to take anyone out riding. I can't figure any of it.

"Buc is going to take you into the train. He'll be along soon."

Leanna went in to wash her hands and hang up the apron Millie had insisted she wear. She moved her luggage downstairs.

While Buc was putting Leanna's belongings in the van, she and Millie stood facing each other, clasping hands. Not a word was exchanged. Then Leanna turned away saying, "I'll write, okay."

She slid into the passenger side and couldn't look back. Buc seemed to sense her mood, and they rode in silence.

When they arrived at the depot he carried her things inside. Leanna seated herself in the dimly lit, dusty building. She sat there alone on the old-fashioned, pew-like wooden benches. She felt like every ounce of energy had been drained from her. Thinking to herself, A woman your age shouldn't cry over something that didn't really happen. But her heart knew that it did happen, on her part.

After seeing that Leanna was situated, Buc left to move the car into a parking space. When he reappeared she was surprised. "You shouldn't have to sit here by yourself," he proclaimed.

They were waiting by the tracks when the train pulled in. "Thanks a lot for bringing me in, Buc."

"I asked for the privilege. I've enjoyed your being here, we all have."

"All aboard!"

Leanna gave Buc a quick hug, which was readily returned. Her last words to him before climbing up the steps were, "Take care of everyone for me."

Her compartment was on the side of the depot. Buc waited until the train pulled out. He took his hat off and waved. She waved until the station was lost in darkness.

As Buc walked to the van he was shaking his head and wondering, Where in the devil is Sam?

 CHAPTER 19

Sam sat at the breakfast table, unshaven and looking tired. He was telling Millie about the hunt. "The most deceptive lion I've ever dealt with. It even had Big John puzzled a time or two. It's the dogs that do the work. He has the best-trained animals I've ever seen. We have to give them the credit of the showdown.

"Afterward we ended up at his place. We had something to eat, and I fell asleep on his davenport. I didn't even hear his little one nor the TV. Finally, when he and his wife turned in they woke me and sent me home. I don't even know what time it was. Where's my girl this morning?"

Millie looked over her shoulder. "You talkin' about Leanna? Wipe that foolish look off your face. She's probably one-third of the way home by now."

Sam looked stricken and laid his fork down.

Millie returned to concentrating on some pans in the dishwater, chatting away. "She's had a fine time her last couple of days."

"She and LC took a picnic and went for an all-day ride. She was flushed when they got back; all that fresh air. Plus, they ran across some rustlers."

"Tim and Randy invited her to go to the rodeo but she was so tired from the day before that she went with Fred and me later on in the day.

She came home wound up with excitement. She got a taste of it and has promised Tim she'd go with him some time when she comes to visit the kids."

"Buc drove her to the train and saw her off. According to him, she gave him a hug and asked him to look after everyone. He didn't leave until . . ."

Before she had finished the sentence the door slammed so hard it jarred every dish in the cupboards. Millie smiled. How could such a smart man be so stupid? Did he just expect Leanna to forget her return ticket and dally around in case he wanted to spend time with her? Men!

She didn't see his boots for two days. One of the lads said he came to the barn, saddled his horse, and rode out. Never spoke to a soul, took no food or water.

When he again placed his feet under the kitchen table he looked haggard. Millie was full of advice she wanted to give him, and it was hard to keep her tongue still. Repeatedly she wished to say, "Go get her, Sam, and bring her home."

After a few days Sam seemed to be his old self. But he couldn't hide his restlessness. He was often short with folks, even some of the guests, which was out of character for him.

The porter on the train had Leanna's bed put together in no time. She was surprised that she went to sleep at all, but she slept soundly until morning.

Working her way to the dining car, she heard the whistle blow. She liked the staccato noise made by the rails as she walked between cars. She enjoyed her breakfast and visiting with other travelers.

When she returned to her sleeper accommodations she found her bed folded up. Leanna liked the closeness of the little private room.

Opening her purse she got her small calendar out. She and Cindy had left home on Tuesday, July 1st, arriving in Texas that Thursday noon. It was now Friday, July 18th. She'd be home tomorrow evening, late. She had asked for the whole month off so she could get her life back to normal again.

Was that what she wanted now? She had always looked forward to vacations and equally forward to returning home. This time was so different. She thought about Millie and each individual on the ranch, trying hard not to separate Sam from the rest.

Tomorrow she would be in Chicago, so she had all of today to think and put her thoughts back in the proper perspective. She needed this day.

How could her feeling about life, and herself, change so drastically in two and a half weeks? She knew in her heart that she had not only fallen in love with Sam, she had also acquired feelings for west Texas. Why? It was almost desolate compared to where she had always lived. Ah, the mysteries of life.

Her mind began to drift. She thought about how, as we go through life, we begin to realize that there is a limit to allotted time for some things. Sometimes we forget who we are. We begin to over-rate ourselves, to think everything is going our way. It's the same thing that happens to movie stars and sports figures.

It takes little to make us aware of the fact that none of it is true; that there are insincere people surrounding us.

There's always the front man, who is kind, polite, and full of promises. Then there's the one who has to tell us the truth. It is an old game that will be played until the end of time.

How often we are fooled and we try and hide our embarrassment of being caught up in the shell game. Gullibility, it makes the world go 'round.

Life is full of carnivals. Beware of the pitch man. He lures you into a trap. Enjoy the bright lights, but do not be blinded by them.

You feel sorry for your lack of confidence in yourself. "He likes me best. I'm special." Child's thinking. It's really business as usual.

When you are standing in front of them you have their undivided attention. They smile, laugh, listen, answer questions. They offer to do things for you. It's like a receiving line; you must enjoy that pleasurable contact, because then it is someone else's turn.

She felt that it was more than kindness. Something had been stirred in her that had been idle for a number of years. The foolishness of a girl. A flutter that should have been forbidden. A reckless dreamer.

There was a soft tap on her door. "Yes."

The porter slid the door and stuck his head through. "Where's that happy-go-lucky lady that made the trip out with us?"

"She's trying to think, and figure out the rest of her life. "

"They made the last call for lunch, could I get you something?"

"You know, I would like a glass of iced tea."

When the young man returned he was carrying a small tray.

"Oh, how refreshing that looks. Tea, cheese, crackers, and fruit. I appreciate it."

"You know I copied down a saying just last week, 'You plan, and God laughs.'"

Leanna smiled. "You are wise beyond your years."

With that he slid the door shut.

Females let their imaginations run in the wrong direction. Of course everyone was nice. Unless she was a real nasty, there was no way anyone would treat the mother of the bride with disrespect. Keep her happy, then send her home. Now you are getting nasty, Leanna, and inappreciative. It's my own fault that I took things differently than they were meant. Shame, shame. My daughter has married into a fine family. I am so thankful for that.

Having sorted it through to her satisfaction, she dozed for a while. Then she walked down to the observation car to socialize.

• • •

One evening, at the table, everyone was inquiring whether there had been any word from Leanna. Had she gotten home okay and how she was doing? Gramps piped up and said, "I know Cindy was too young for me; and already spoken for. But that mother of hers is a humdinger, too. I think she and I could have worked something out. Buc's got himself a young friend and they're hittin' it off good."

Sam nearly choked on his coffee. He got up from the table. Walking behind Gramps' chair he sounded angry when he blurted out, "You're too old for her." He left the room grumbling to himself.

Gramps stared after him. "What's his problem?"

No one said a word.

No one had heard harsh words pass between the two before.

 CHAPTER 20

It was the 28th of July when Cindy pulled up in front of the hotel. She looked up, and there, framed in the screened window, was her friend, Conner.

"Conner, after a couple of weeks of marriage my husband kissed me this morning and said he still loved me. So, I'm feeling pretty frisky today. You've got pictures to show me?"

"Come on up." As Cindy walked through the door he said, "The look on your face is a picture of happiness."

"Let me have a good look at you, Conner. You still have that full blond head of hair, those blue eyes that look like they understand me. Tall, so you can observe things better than the rest of us. You are hiding your smile. Are you not happy with your world?"

He took her hand. "If you are happy with what I have for you, then I will smile. Here's a box of photos. We'll go through them and see what you think."

Conner would say nothing of the folder of pictures he had put in the back of his closet. They were so revealing that he would not dare show them to anyone.

They were shots of Sam and Leanna. The camera had picked up

something that he was sure no one was aware of, not even the participants. When they had come through the developing process he lined them up and sat in his work chair to study them.

At times when they were included in the same picture Leanna would be interacting with several guests, but Sam's eyes were focusing on her alone. Sam would be shaking hands with friends, but Leanna was solely seeing him.

He had seen these looks in his parents' eyes, over the years. Many words passed through his thoughts, but the one that kept reappearing was . . . love. He didn't believe that either of them knew what the other was experiencing. What a discovery. Was he the only one who knew?

"Here's Mom and me getting off the train; and me nearly knocking Jimmy off his feet, I was so glad to see him.

"Blaze leaning over the corral gate and Dancer looking up to him." Cindy studied the picture. "When was this taken?"

"You talked to me in April, about the job, and I started in May. Often it was pure luck. The right place at the right time."

"Some good shots of the guests, mingling. My mom and me looking around in my school room.

"Here's the church. Wonderful coverage of the flowers." Cindy started to laugh. "Some fun ones of the locals and their reactions to the transition of their little church.

"Oh look, Millie with her apron on in the ranch kitchen. Then her and Fred dancing at the wedding. I bet they'd like one of each of those. Millie will fuss about the one but Fred will love it.

"The boys hanging around the barn in their work clothes. Then all duded up for the wedding; better have a copy of that one. We'll put it up in their work area to shock them.

"Here's Mother and me racing the horses toward that tree. You're a crazy man, Conner." She looked up at him with a twinkle in her eye.

"Looks like you've done what I wanted.

"Gramps at the wedding, all spiffed up, dancing with the ladies. Oh, look at this, him working with the horses early in the morning. I like that. That's him in my book.

"The Michigan girls coming down the aisle. Better mail them each a copy.

"Then Mother. Me, too. Mmmm."

Conner looked solemn. "Had to catch a few traditionals."

"Nice one of Taylor. Now, here's a couple of neat ones. Taylor in her waitress uniform; busy at work. Her racing into the ranch yard and meeting my mom for the first time. You are a sneak Conner. How did you get some of these with out people realizing it?"

"A zoom lens and peeking around corners."

"Do the town folks know you peek around corners?" Conner just laughed. "I try and keep that my secret. Seriously, I don't normally do such things."

"I said I didn't want any extra pictures and already I've mentioned a few. Better have the ones of Taylor in her work outfit and wedding outfit in a double frame. From what I hear, Jeremy would like to have those.

"Hey! Sam, Jimmy, and the three groomsmen in their sharp outfits. A good looking bunch!"

Cindy paused and studied Conner. He was beginning to relax. He had obviously been worried about her reaction to the pictures. Maybe she had scared him by all of her odd ideas. He had done a super job.

The next photo stopped her cold. "How did you do this?"

"You may have forgotten but after speaking to each of your guests you and Jimmy stepped outside to get a breath of air. The deer and trees in the hazy background are the ones that appeared that day you helped me lug my camera equipment into the woods."

"Remarkable." Cindy couldn't take her eyes from the setting; it fascinated her.

"Oh look, Sam and Jimmy in their work clothes, leaning on the fence. Each in deep thought. I wonder what they were thinking about? I shall have to ask them to see if they recall. Then again, maybe I should not.

"LC and Buc, working on fence posts. It's so good, and natural looking. I need an enlargement to hang in my hallway. I think a lot of these two. I'll probably want some others, too."

When she looked at the last picture the color faded from her cheeks. Conner didn't know what to think. She studied it very carefully. She took a shallow breath and spoke softly. "I will need a very large one of this and it must be in a beautiful frame."

Conner stepped to his closet and returned with the finished product, framed appropriately. He rested it on her knees and held the top steady.

Cindy slid away into a private sanctuary. Slowly, her fingers traced the figures in the piece. She was amazed. It was almost like a painting. It was her life, her future. It almost seemed alive. She and Jimmy were in everyday riding clothes. Cindy tried to recall the day. They stood next to each other, casually; and their love was so plain. Dancer was lying by their feet. Behind them was an outline of a pick-up truck. In the distance was Buffer racing to join them.

Cindy leaned back. Conner quickly moved the photograph, leaning it against a chair. He thought she was going to faint. When he turned back she was crying.

"I'm so sorry; I wanted to do something special. Instead, I've upset you." He didn't know what to do. Finally, he sat next to her and held her in his arms. He was crushed. His good intentions had backfired.

Cindy looked up at him with the tears still tumbling from her eye lashes. "My dear, sweet Conner. I cannot believe what you have done. The pictures well surpass my wishes.

"This last one has undone the new bride emotionally. If I was not already married I would run off with the likes of you. Can you find me a box of tissues so I can pull myself together? I have never seen such work."

They still sat side by side. Conner jumped up in awkwardness. They both laughed, a nervous laugh like people do in such situations.

"While I'm vulnerable present me with your bill."

Conner took it from the desk drawer and hesitatingly gave it to Cindy.

She glanced at it and wrote a check out for triple the amount. "Never undercharge, Conner; it's bad for business."

He stood staring at the check.

"You need to go on to school; not for photography but for business practices. What you have done is incredible. You underestimate your ability. You put your heart in this. Never change.

"I need to take these home and show Jimmy. I'll get back to you on what I want done. I'll pay additional for that, of course. Help me carry the big one to the car."

As they passed through the lobby Cindy called out at the top of her lungs, "Mrs. O'Malley, your son is a genius."

 # CHAPTER 21

July 29

Dear Mom,

We got back okay. That sweet husband of mine had made arrangements at a local bed and breakfast. He figured it would be more pleasant for me than walking into the unsettled little house. We did not arrive until dark and I appreciated the thoughtfulness.

He finally confessed that the idea came from Aunt Millie. What would we all do without her? She quietly does so many important little things. Slips them in in such a way that I don't believe she realizes what a helpful person she is.

I'm glad I didn't approach the house until the next morning. There were some brands of varmints that were unknown to me. Sand had blown in around the windows. Keeping the place decent will be a full-time job.

I have not purchased the stuff for the bedroom yet. I want it to be just right. You know how silly new brides are. But there are nice new sheets and blankets on the bed. Even Jimmy seems to enjoy the improvement. He keeps telling people that I am a better housekeeper than he was. I have no intention of denying that. It won't be kept up quite so well I'm afraid once school begins.

Jimmy is gone a lot. So much work at the ranch. His dad is spending serious time with him now that Jimmy has settled down. Sam wants him to work more and more toward taking over.

LC informed us that our Dancer is expecting. No one is sure what the combination will be. She got out of the barn one night. We'll have her spayed after. She'll be a good mama. I'll send pictures. We wanted to move Dancer to our house but decided against it. She's so happy at the ranch. It would prove lonely for her here.

I haven't been by to work on my school room yet. Am anxious to get at it. I'd like to come up with something to offer my students that is new.

Yesterday I went to Conner's and picked up the pictures. Oh, Mom, he did it for me. They are exceptional. I'll send a few. The rest we can enjoy together the first time you visit. I need some time to settle in.

The first time I went to the grocery to buy supplies I nearly ran into Mrs. Taylor with my cart. I was about to apologize when she scooted away like those strange bugs in my house when I get the broom out. I would like to try and like her but somehow my tolerance level registers pretty low when I deal with her. She seems very odd. Her eyes are shifty. Her pointed nose reminds me of a rat. I better change the subject. Thinking about her gives me the creeps.

I'm so thankful that I have such a loving, normal mother. We get along remarkably well. Taylor sure got short-changed.

How are your flowers? Bet you had some big-time weeding when you got home. Will it seem good to get back to the old routine at work?

In the future we'll build a home on the ranch land somewhere. It will be fun to plan. Maybe fun isn't a good word. I've heard that a lot of arguments come with that project. You may not hear from me for a bit. I wanted to get this in the mail before I rolled my sleeves up and dug in.

Love you lots

Cindy and Jimmy

 CHAPTER 22

The 2nd of September, an overdue letter arrived addressed to Millie. Leanna was writing to thank everyone for their many kindnesses. Millie had a feeling that Leanna had wanted to use more words than she did. It was not just a basic thank you; but then maybe she was reading too much between the lines.

Later in the day as she read it aloud to Sam, he remarked, "Seems awfully formal."

That did it.

Millie lashed out at him, "Did you expect her to write and admit how much she cares for you? How hard it was for her to return to Michigan? Why don't you bring her back here where she belongs? Then this place would be a home again, not just a working ranch full of grumpy hard-workin' cowboys: and city dudes who wanna be cowboys." She gasped and her hand hastily covered her mouth.

With relief she saw the creases around Sam's eyes, and a slow smile develop.

"Where have you been, sister of mine? I've needed help bad." Sam rose from the table and patted her shoulder. He didn't shut the door to his study, and she overheard him making flight arrangements.

He hurried up the stairs. Minutes later he came down with his suitcase. "I'll see what I can do, Mil," and he kissed her on the cheek. He called the barns, and one of the boys would drive him in to the airport.

"This may be the scariest deal I ever made. It may not go easy. I'm not sure when I'll return. I'll give it my best. I love her, Mil. I want her real bad."

"You tell her this time. Don't take it for granted that she knows."

She went to the porch as they pulled out. She wished him well. The two of them will be back soon, she thought. At the same time she balled up her fists because she couldn't cross that many fingers. Then she looked up to the sky. "I think it would be the best thing in the world for both of them. What do you think?"

Fred came up behind her. "Who you talkin' to, woman?"

"A good friend."

• • •

After Labor Day the kids were sitting in their seats at school in new jeans and T-shirts. No voices echoed through the mall, so lots of employees, from different stores, were given the option of a few days off. Leanna was taking from Wednesday the 3rd through Sunday the 7th.

She had decided to take advantage of the spectacular September weather. Cleaning out her flower beds wasn't as exciting as the spring work. Then, you uncovered so many surprises under the pine needles and dried leaves. She had been putting the chore off and now needed to hustle before the cold set in.

Rounding up her oldest clothes, she covered her exterior with bug and sun goop. By mid-afternoon the dirt was clinging to her face and hands. She had tucked her pant legs into holey kneesocks to keep mosquitoes from biting her legs.

The hard work and what it accomplished made her feel satisfied. She loosened the tie of her sun hat and lay back in the dirt. The hat, out of shape after years of gardening, was resting on her face to protect her eyes from the sun. It was a good-feeling day. Life had its seasons. Accepting that was half the battle.

"Beg pardon."

Leanna jolted to a sitting position. Using her hand to shade her eyes, she squinted to identify the figure standing at the back door of her garage.

"Well, if it isn't Samuel James Pride himself. Come sit yourself on the grass and tell me all the news. I'm just the gardener here, but I'll see that it gets passed on to the lady of the house."

After Sam had caught her up with a report, he sat and enjoyed her presence. The fresh air felt good after the plane ride and his sleepless night in a motel in Grand Rapids. "You look great, Leanna."

She burst out laughing. "I'm filthy and I smell bad."

"That's the part that's scary. You still look good to me."

Leanna let that statement glide by without putting much emphasis on it.

She rose reaching for his hand. "Come on inside. You can relax. That will give me an opportunity to shower and get cleaned up. Then I'll make us some lemonade. You can then tell me why you are in this part of the country; and why you didn't inform me of your arrival."

When Leanna came back into the living room she found Sam asleep on the couch. It made her feel good that he could relax in her presence and her home.

Moving to the kitchen she stirred up the lemonade. She went ahead and added the ice upon hearing stretching noises. Placing a few butter cookies on that colorful little plate that had been her grandmother's—after all she did have a special caller—she carried the tray into the room.

Looking at him she began to smile. His short nap had produced a tuft of hair sticking up like Alfalfa's in the Little Rascals. "Would you like to sit on the back porch?"

"Let's stay in here," he replied.

After a few swallows, Leanna began to converse. "I didn't realize you did any business with people in this part of the country. Or is this a stop off on the way to somewhere?"

Sam looked at her solemnly. "I came here purposely." There was a pause and then he continued. "I came to ask you to marry me."

Leanna, with a cookie halfway to her mouth, held it in midair and stared at him. She couldn't move. Her mind refused to function. Was this a dream? The body she occupied must belong to someone else. She looked away from the person who had spoken. What had he asked her? Did she know him? Laying the cookie down she looked out toward the porch. She was stunned. Confused. Dazed. This couldn't be real. Her insides began to churn. If only she could get her thinking process under control.

Observing that blank stare, Sam stood and picked up his hat. He walked to Leanna, tipped up her chin and brushed her lips with his. "I guess I misunderstood, and I've made a terrible mistake." He held his hat in both hands. "Forgive me. I hope we can still be friends."

Leanna heard the door click shut. That clicking sound broke through the barrier. She felt like her heart was being run through a shredder.

Running to the door, she grabbed the knob. The door flew open and hit the door stop. Her voice cried out in anguish, "No! No." Her arms were outstretched. "Sam, don't go," she pleaded.

He turned, and with few strides was in the house. Kicking the door closed with his heel, he had Leanna in his arms. He was kissing her face, her eyelids, her neck. She was shaking.

"You're all I've thought of since returning. Teach me to love again, Sam."

With those words he took her hand and they moved to the couch. "Was that a yes?"

She reached up and touched his face. "I love you so very much."

"When I met you at the train, it was at my son's insistence. At first, I panicked, thinking you were that stern-looking inebriated woman sitting in the station."

Leanna began to laugh. "I thought you were the skinny sickly man coming out of the restroom."

Then they were both laughing.

"When you walked up, Leanna, and linked your arm in mine, admitting your uneasiness, I began to love you at that very moment."

"One stipulation to this marriage thing."

"Mmm, and what would that be?"

"If I marry you, you have to teach me to jingle, and allow me to do it."

"You drive a hard bargain. So, would you be marrying me because you like my horses, or because you like me? I don't want to be number two on your list. If that's the deal, I don't want to be married.

"I also didn't come all this way to play lengthy games. I have a ranch to run. I want to take you home as my wife."

"You're sure of it?"

"Yes, Ma'am. I size people up pretty fast. But if you aren't sure, in your heart . . . Boy, it's been a long time since I've dealt with a woman and her feelings."

"After being on the ranch I have felt that my life, the way I was living it, was so senseless. I've missed you terribly. You see, at first I thought we had something going. Then I thought I was being a fool; that you were just being nice to me."

"I'm not that nice to anyone." He grabbed her and pulled her to him.

"I can't say I haven't had a woman since my wife's death. But there was never any love involved. The ones that seemed interested in me caused no real spark. I even tried a couple of times to let it happen. They were nice women."

"But it was easy for me to get sidetracked by life at the ranch, so I knew it wouldn't flourish. I'm devoted to the ranch, but a woman needs to be loved completely. Love can't be an afterthought."

"I don't know as I have what it takes to be a rancher's wife."

"You've caught me at a good time in my life. My hard-working days are over. Now I hire younger people who have more energy. I'm preparing Jimmy to take over complete management, in time.

"And, by golly, now that I've got you to jingle I can really take it easy.

"I've been mean and ornery ever since you left. Just ask Millie. She said it was the first time she'd ever seen a prize cow slip out of my rope and get away.

"If it's a deal; no traveling under two names. You go home with me as my wife. I've waited a long time for you and I didn't even know I was looking. If you're not interested I'll turn and go back now. To tell you the truth, I'd rather stay here and make love to you, just to see if I remembered how."

"They say it's like riding a bicycle. Is this a business deal? You are handling it like one. I bet you buy steers and heifers and horses the same way."

"I'd like to get sentimental and romantic with you but . . . I guess I honestly don't want either of us to get hurt. It hasn't got so involved yet that either of us can't walk away and survive.

"I love you. I didn't think you would leave like that. I know, I was being thoughtless. It won't be easy. We are each set in our ways. But I'll give it everything I've got. And from what I gathered I'd say you would do the same.

"I'm going to a motel. I'll be back in two hours. If you'd at least like to talk about it, we'll go out to someplace nice for supper. If it's a no, well, just leave the house dark and don't answer the door." He walked out the door and slammed it.

The door swung open equally as fast. "No!"

He stood there like a statue.

"You are not going to stay in a motel. You'll stay here, where you belong. We'll give it a couple of days. If we go back together we'll go as husband and wife. I love you more than you can imagine, cowboy. Come back in and sit a spell."

He took her arm and pushed her back inside. The door slid shut. He removed his hat and folded her into his arms. He kissed her until her legs felt like rubber bands, and she lost her senses. Finally, he pulled away and guided her back to the couch. She sat there shaking her head. He sat grinning at her.

She grabbed his hat from the floor, slapped it on her head, and made a statement. "I love a man with spunk."

Supper was forgotten. Their hunger had nothing to do with food.

The bicycle theory was proven right once again.

Leanna proved to him that it was not his horses that would be her number one interest. Sam proved to her that whatever uncertainty they had to work through, they would do it together.

When they woke in the morning, Leanna sat up with a start. "I must look horrid."

"Well." With that he pulled her up against his bare chest. "Don't back out on me now, lady."

She snuggled up against him, with a deep sigh.

Later, when they were up and dressed and Leanna had fixed breakfast, she looked at him and said, "We do have some serious talking to do."

She went to her desk and picked up a big yellow tablet and a pen.

"How much time do you have?"

"I can be gone a while but not too long. Jimmy isn't ready for the whole burden of the ranch to be put on his shoulders yet. Of course, LC and Buc will help him."

"What about the marriage itself?"

"I haven't got anything to do this afternoon."

"Be serious."

"I am. The sooner, the better. I don't want to be someone who just wandered into your yard. Plus I don't want to give you an opportunity to change your mind."

"I know there will be documents needed. I brought the necessary ones."

Leanna folded her arms across her chest. "Were you that sure of yourself?"

"No, but one always goes to a meeting prepared, according to what I checked on, the three-day waiting period can be waived by the county clerk for a $5 fee. You could get us an appointment with your family doctor today. We need rings. Can do that this morning. Minister, two witnesses. That should solve that problem. Tomorrow or the next day should do it."

Leanna sat with her mouth open. Shaking her head she complained, "I thought the woman planned the wedding."

"Time is of the essence. And there's other things to take care of. I'm trying to sweep you off your feet as far as the wedding itself goes."

"Stop. Day after tomorrow. I need a suitable dress and a fancy nightie. You are not going to run the whole show."

"Women!" Sam pinched her cheek.

"There's my job."

"We'll drive over there tomorrow and you can give them the scoop."

"House."

"We'll make an appointment with a realtor and let him, or her, take care of all details."

"Furniture?"

"If there are pieces you want, we'll make arrangements for a moving van."

"How do we get back to Texas?"

"You're wording that wrong; 'How do we get home?' That's up to you."

Leanna made a face. "Lucky me. Let's go by train. It will give us a couple of quiet days. We'll need them."

"I'll make arrangements."

"One request. Could we take two or three days after the wedding, and all arrangements are worked out, and honeymoon in Michigan? I'd like to show you where I have spent my life. We may never return here. It's pretty this time of year."

"Request granted. Sounds like a grand idea. Then take the train on home."

Leanna put her elbow on the table and rested her chin in her hand. "Gosh, home. You've got my head spinning, Sam."

"I just remembered something. In August, there was an Amtrak train wreck near Kingman, Arizona. A bridge shifted because of heavy rains the night before and caused a derailment. No deaths or critically injured, but dozens hurt. Will we be safe?"

"We don't go through Arizona to get to Texas from here."

"I know but . . ."

Sam looked at her and smiled. "You don't think I'm going to go to all this trouble and not take my prize home, do you? Mustn't worry. You're safe with me. I'll look after you."

"Oh, my. We had better call the kids."

That evening they called the little rental house, but no answer. So Sam put a call through to the ranch. Jimmy answered on the office phone.

Sam told him the details of what was to happen, and asked him to have Cindy call home so she and Leanna could talk.

There was a long silence on the ranch end, almost as if the phone line had gone dead. "Dad, there's a problem."

"What's the matter?"

"No trouble at the ranch. It's Cindy. Millie told me where you had gone. I gave Cindy the news, thinking she would be excited. She's acted strange ever since. Sad, distressed. For some reason she's fighting this union. Never mentions Leanna anymore, acts as if she doesn't exist. I am totally puzzled. Not really sure how to handle it. I'll pass on the good news; sincere congratulations on my part. But I don't think she'll call. Can you handle it on that end?"

Leanna frowned, but there was so many things whirling through her mind that the disappointment of not being able to share this joy with her daughter was soon lost in the shuffle.

 CHAPTER 23

On September 11th, at 8:30 in the morning, Mr. and Mrs. Samuel Pride were boarding the train for Chicago. This was not Leanna's favorite part of the trip. She became restless on the three-hour ride, in coach, to the big city.

There would be the six-hour wait, and maybe, longer, for the sleeper. Although there were things to occupy the time, people-watching was her favorite; she liked to get started on the main part of the journey. Leanna liked the comfort of staying put for two days.

When she and Sam were settled in for the night she started to giggle, trying to muffle the sound with her pillow.

"Now what?"

"I didn't take your size into consideration. The bathroom and sink arrangement are not a bit convenient for you."

To quiet her laughing he kissed her soundly. "I'll survive," he whispered.

After returning from breakfast the following morning, Sam slipped his shoes off. Propping the pillows in the corner he made himself comfortable. "This marriage business tuckers me out." The movement of the train put him to sleep in short order.

Leanna sat in the chair across, watching out the window. July 1st she and Cindy had left for Texas. It was now September 12th and she and Sam were heading for the same destination. Three months time, what drastic changes had befallen her. For a number of years things had moved along smoothly, like the clattering train. One major adjustment would be the need for more flexibility.

She became aware of Sam's reflection in the window. Mr. Tough Cowboy, with a heart that wouldn't fit into a bushel basket.

That reminded her of some things she had hastily packed into boxes to be moved. There were her basket-making supplies, one of the hobbies she enjoyed. It had seemed important; maybe it was just part of clinging to the past. Her time would be taken up with new interests; and always first would be Sam. All those years of surviving alone had left an empty space in her being. A wave of happiness swept through her.

The house, job, everything came back to mind. All organized so fast. Leanna's car had been sold to a neighbor boy for transportation back and forth to the university. She hoped they hadn't left anything undone. There was always the phone and mail service. Even the thought of it all left her exhausted.

The train stopped at a small town. Leanna watched as a young man stepped down unto the platform. The family waited. He hurried up to them. His mother picked invisible lint from his Navy uniform. The desire to wrap her arms around him showed in her eyes. Grown-up boys. Could he feel her tenderness? A glimpse of U.S.A., by train. One must store scenes like that. It helps to pad the heart when things go wrong.

All of a sudden Leanna straightened and pulled back from the window. For one instant the face of Mrs. Taylor had appeared in the glass. It seemed so real that Leanna looked toward the door to see if she stood there.

Sam sat watching her. "Come sit next to me. What startled you?"

"Mrs. Taylor's face reflected in the window glass. It was so clear." Leanna quickly moved next to Sam. "It gave me a chill."

"She can do nothing to hurt you. I won't let anyone hurt you."

Leanna leaned back against him, moving his arms around her. Her newfound security blanket. "You can't protect me from life. But I love you for wanting to try."

To change the subject, she brought up the jingle project again. "I'm sure you won't have time to train me. But you can assign me to someone with patience. I know it will take a long time. I want to be able to help, and I'd love to do that. No fooling around, I'm talking hard experience. Not being in the way, but really good help. I'm determined to do it. And then . . . "

"There's more?"

"When I really am good at it, I'd like a cowboy hat and boots."

"Why don't we just go to the saddlery and get you your boots and hat?"

She looked insulted. "No, sir, I have to earn them."

Sam wrapped his arms around her again and pulled her back against him. "Leanna, there's something I have to tell you." There was such a change in his tone that she tried to move away so she could look into his face. Holding her fast he continued. "That night I talked to Jimmy on the phone; there is a problem."

With that Leanna did pull away. It sounded like this should be directed to her square on, not from behind her back.

"Millie had indicated to Jimmy where I was going and why. There were lots of questions because I left in such a hurry. She thought it was important that he know the score."

"He passed the information on to Cindy. He said it was like she pulled a window shade down between them. He cannot figure out what's going on. When he attempted to talk to her about it, to bring it out in the open; she just looked at him. She is holding something inside.

"He said they get along just fine as long as your existence isn't acknowledged. If he mentions anything about our marrying, she walks away as if he hasn't spoken."

Leanna's shoulders sagged. "I haven't a clue. You should see the loving letter she sent at the end of the month. In my wildest imagination, I come up empty."

Sam put his hand on hers. "Listen to me. We can do nothing until we arrive, then we'll try and sort it out. Don't let it ruin this short time we have alone. I didn't want you walking into the situation cold. Maybe there's a simple explanation, a misunderstanding.

"When we do get home I will have a lot to do. I won't be able to spend this kind of time with you. It won't be that I love you less."

Leanna let a small laugh escape.

"Did I say something funny?"

"Cindy and I had this same talk on our way out. She labeled it our mother-daughter talk. Even though I am older and supposedly wiser, I probably needed the same talk. I'm sure there will be times when I question this plan. It will be true on your part also. So let's pretend we are true newlyweds and don't have a care in the world. Whaddaya say, pardner? Let's lighten up a bit."

The dining host seated them across from a young couple. They had barely sat down when the young lady gushed out the news. "We are on our honeymoon."

"Well," said Leanna, placing her hand lightly on Sam's leg, "So are we."

As the women bubbled with the coincidence, Sam's intake of air was overlooked. He was thankful for that. This man-and-woman thing was still a bit new, after many years of nonparticipation. This woman beside him had jump-started his dead battery.

He raised his water goblet for a toast. "To each of us, many years of happiness."

The young man took a sigh of relief and started confessing to Sam. "I was worried. Thought maybe I should offer to buy champagne. Three problems with that. We are nondrinkers, I think champagne tastes like sparkling vinegar, and I'm running low on funds."

The meal was good and the laughter was the best medicine for Leanna.

Sam had called the ranch when the arrival by train was finalized. One of the boys was to drive the van in and leave it, as train times were not usually according to schedule.

They had loaded their things into the van and just left the station when Leanna realized that Sam was preoccupied with the truck in front of them.

The truck slammed on its breaks at the light, and a dog came tumbling out of the truck bed, rolled and hit the light pole on the corner. The driver jumped from the truck, picked the dog up with a struggle; the animal yelping with each move. He placed the dog in the cab and scurried back into the driver's side and drove to the next corner.

A red light. Sam was out of the van and standing next to the driver's window, in an instant. Sam told Leanna months later that the dog was whining and cried out in pain when he recognized him.

"You work for the Pride Ranch, young man?"

"Yeah, whatever it says on the truck."

Sam doubted that.

"The dog's just a mutt, no big loss."

Sam nearly tore the door handle off. He took hold of the man's collar, dragging him from the cab.

"I don't even dare think of what I'd like to do to you."

A police car pulled up beside them. Sam handed the man over to the officer. "I suspect he's stolen one of our trucks. He claims he works for the ranch. If so, he's just been fired. I've got to get the dog to the vet."

He walked back to the van and told Leanna to drive on to the ranch. When he glanced in the rearview mirror he saw that instead she was right behind him. She was not going to be easy to handle. The thought made him smile, in spite of the situation they were in at the moment. Gently his hand rested on the injured dog's head.

The vet checked the dog over carefully. "Sorry, Sam, he's got a broken back."

Leanna's stomach wrenched. She could see what this was doing to Sam. Moving in next to him she took his hand.

He acknowledged her touch with a squeeze. He then gently picked up the old dog and held him while the vet prepared the shot. Then he carefully carried him out and laid him on the cab seat again.

Leanna drove the balance of the way to her new home with tears streaming down her cheeks.

The two vehicles steered their miniature parade past the ranch house. In a field not far from the house, in the midst of some trees, Sam stopped the truck. He reached in the back for the shovel that was always kept there. The hole was dug and the big brown dog was put to rest.

Sam and Leanna paused side by side, holding hands. Nothing was said. She was sure that this was not a normal procedure on a ranch. This animal had to have captured a piece of this man's heart.

They turned and Sam walked her to the van. He took her in his arms and with a choked voice whispered, "I love you." He then held the door for her to get into the seat. If there had been an ounce of indecision on her part about this union, it was erased with the sharing of these past moments. Oh, how she loved this man: big in stature, kindness in his heart, and willing to share his way of life and love with her.

The vet had thought to call the ranch, so everyone knew that the arrival of the couple would be different than originally planned.

When they entered the house, Millie and Fred were there, and things were subdued. They had a light supper.

Fred and Sam retired to the office to bring things up to date. "Not much of a homecoming for you, Leanna. Do you feel abandoned?"

"On the contrary, Millie. The episode made me feel very much a part of life here. I had been concerned about the adjustment. I'm not anymore. It will take some doing but the pattern will develop sooner than I thought."

"Fred and I moved back to our place because this is your home now."

Leanna stopped right there and expressed some feeling. She felt that the four of them needed to sit and talk to decide the best situation for all. Things had to be carefully thought through. Her desire for a smooth changeover was strong. But Millie was the one person that she thought she could safely put on hold for a few days. Millie would understand.

Millie took Leanna upstairs to show her the room she had done over for the new circumstances.

"Oh, Millie, it's lovely. Not too masculine, nor too feminine. Thank you so much. You're a dear, especially to do it in such a short time. I hadn't even thought about it."

"You can change it to your liking from here, but I thought it was a beginning."

"I'm very tired. Going to turn in. Sunrise will come soon enough. Tomorrow I begin a new role. I must learn how to be a rancher's wife."

An hour later, Sam softly closed the door. Leanna had left the bedside lamp on. She had fallen asleep.

A wife in his bed. She was his, and he loved her.

It was the night that Leanna found out what true love was all about. Sam woke her gently. She smiled, then moved into his arms. "We're home, Sam."

That ended any conversation. Their passion was uncontrollable. Early in the morning, before the sun had made its way above the mountains, they made love again. This time it was slow, deliberate, and wonderful.

When Leanna shook herself awake at 6:00, Sam's side of the bed was empty. She hurriedly showered and dressed. Running down the stairs she hustled into the kitchen. He had started the coffee.

"I've only been down here a few minutes, if that's what all the hurry is about. You can get breakfast going. I've got to talk to one of the boys." As he passed her he patted her backside. "You're doin' fine, sweetheart."

"Get on outta here, silly."

When the door opened again, Sam's comment was, "Just as I thought, no new hands have been hired."

Later that day, the sheriff stopped by. Seems the kid had escaped from a jail downstate. He was stealing transportation, ditching it, then stealing again, as a means of getting away. He didn't know the dog was asleep in the back. Said he was sorry about the dog.

Sam put his arm around Leanna's shoulder and introduced her.

• • •

That evening just before dusk Leanna heard the horses' hooves in the drive. Sam was riding one and leading another. "Come on, gal. A short ride will do us good." They rode to the top of the hill, like before, to watch the lights come on below. "Welcome home. My biggest desire is to have you be happy here."

After brushing the horses down they walked back to the house together. The evening was getting cold. Sam built a small fire in the fireplace in the parlor. They sat back to back on the big sofa, he reading the paper and Leanna starting a book she had taken from the shelves in the office. He smiled when he noticed her choice: The Horse Whisperer by Nicholas Evans.

• • •

The next morning Leanna received a phone call from Mrs. O'Malley. Would she come for coffee at the hotel? It was rainy and cold and Leanna was glad to get the invitation.

They spoke of small things then Mrs. O'Malley said, "I have something for you." Excusing herself, she stepped into the office and returned with a 9x12 brown clasp envelope.

"I had written to Conner at college telling of your marriage to Sam. He called home and told me where to find this in his room. Said I was to present it to you as a wedding gift."

"Do you know what's in it?"

"For the life of me, I don't."

"What do you say to us having a look together?" Leanna opened the clasp, studied the picture on top, and sat back. Then she placed them all across the big wooden table. The women looked at each other in surprise.

"Conner was aware of what was going on before Sam and I knew it ourselves. No wonder he kept these under wraps. I shall have to write him a thank-you note. An interesting young man. You must be proud of him." They finished the coffee and Leanna hurried home to show the pictures to Sam.

The next three nights Leanna tried to reach Cindy at home. The answering machine's message became dull and insensitive. The only way she knew to put a stop to the problem was to find out what it was. If she let it go, she was afraid it would fester and spread.

Millie and Fred returned to prepare for a small open house for the newly married couple. It was the evening of the 18th, two weeks to the day from when Sam had shown up at Leanna's.

There were enough guests to cover up the fact that Jimmy had arrived alone. He immediately came to Leanna. "I'm sorry. Cindy is home correcting papers. There's a bur under her saddle and she's hurtin' bad. If she'd only talk to me about it."

"It has to come to a head, so we can clear the air."

Just then Sam approached her to introduce a close friend of his that she hadn't met.

• • •

Saturday, Dancer had seven pups. One died, which LC said was common when the mother was young. Leanna wanted so to go take a look, but felt Cindy should have the privilege of seeing them first. Jimmy was as proud as if he had become a father.

By Sunday, she could contain herself no longer. Walking toward the barn she heard voices. Should she go in or not? It was good to hear Cindy's voice, even if it wasn't directed toward her. She was just going to step inside when Cindy brushed past her. She looked at Leanna as if she were a trespassing stranger. Hurrying to her car, she slammed the door, and drove away.

Leanna stood there watching the automobile tear down the driveway. Then she walked into the stall filled with straw. LC was down on his knees. Looking up he said, "It's a fine batch."

Their eyes met and there was understanding. No further comment was made.

Leanna joined him, praising Dancer on her fine job and her new family. "Oh, look at the tiny one off by itself."

"It's the runt. Often they don't make it. Sometimes they just aren't strong enough to fight for their share of milk. This one's pretty quiet. Maybe his spunk will surprise us. Hard to tell."

A few days later, Tinker, Cindy had named him, was wobbly but on his feet and gathering strength.

• • •

It was during this time that Leanna drove into town and stopped at the church. She knocked on the outside door that had OFFICE printed on the window. Trying the knob she stepped in. "Hello."

"I'm back here sorting books."

"Is that you, Tuck?"

A head popped up from some shelving in the back. "What did you say?"

"It is you, good."

The minister looked at her with a puzzled expression. "Who is Tuck? I know you, you're the new Mrs. Pride."

"And I know you. You remind me of Friar Tuck of Sherwood Forest."

He laughed at that. "Would you like to know my given name?"

"No."

"So, then, I must inform my secretary that if a lady's voice asks for Friar Tuck she is to patch her right through."

"Do you have a secretary?"

"No."

Laughter again rang through the dingy cluttered office.

"I should not like to refer to you as Friar Tuck."

"What then?"

"I think of you as just Tuck."

"Then Tuck it shall be. Why am I privileged with this visit? Should I call you Lady Marion?"

"Just plain Leanna will do. A serious problem has developed in our family. I don't know what it is, nor how to solve it. I need someone to talk to. Someone to listen. It's stuffy in here."

"Shall we go for a walk?"

"I'd like that. Can air out the brain that way."

"I assume you are speaking of your daughter's strange behavior."

Leanna looked at him. "Well, it looks like I've come to the right person."

"Don't know as I can help, but I can listen. You aren't letting this interfere with your relationship with Sam, are you? I've observed him for a long time now. Met him in the post office yesterday. Never saw such a wonderful change in a fellow. He needs you, Leanna."

"How do you gather all this information?"

"Just keeping my ears open. I also have a cleaning lady who shows once a week to keep the church tidied up. Any tidbits I miss she picks up and delivers. I'd marry her but she's such a gossip." This was followed with another jovial laugh.

"How come you're not married, Tuck? You seem like such a good sort."

"That's true. In order to be happily married I have to find the other end."

"You've lost me."

"Marriage is like a set of bookends. If they don't match, at least, they must be compatible. I have little to offer."

He linked arms with Leanna and they walked the little path that led up to the cemetery. "Do not be troubled, my child; that's what the priests in the movies always say."

"There's a saying that goes, 'If the problem is too big turn it over to God.' I've done that but . . ."

"And you are no doubt expecting a miracle, pronto. Give Him a chance. So, I am your last resort?"

They were both laughing by this time.

"How about some spicey tea in my sad office?"

"The locals won't spread stories 'bout us, will they? Town minister, of marriageable age, serves spicey tea to another man's new bride."

"Come inside. There's a hot plate in the closet. It makes alarming noises, but it hasn't blown up yet."

The two relaxed over hot tea, and made a pact to become blood brothers, or something like that. When Leanna stepped back outside the sun felt warmer against her skin.

She must remember: first item on her Christmas list, a hot plate, maybe even a two-burner. She felt better. Looking toward the clouds she said, "Please, don't wait too long."

• • •

One of the ranch hands was in town buying his wife a birthday card. As he went to pay, he and the saleslady got to talking about Dancer's litter. "Even though the mother and daughter don't spare a word for each other, they are both crazy about the runt, Tinker. He is a cute little guy."

Further back in the card section stood a woman trying to catch every word. She was clutching her purse with a grip like a hawk that had swooped down on a mouse. Hurrying out the side door and down the street with her head bent, she disappeared.

Later, when the clerk was straightening cards before closing she discovered several cards ripped into pieces and scattered on the floor. Before putting them in the wastebasket she noticed that each had a picture of a puppy on the front. Odd.

 CHAPTER 23

The 1st of the month rolled around before Leanna was able to get to Millie and Fred's. It was on one of those roads that she referred to as treacherous. The locals always laughed when she used the term.

Millie was obviously glad to see her. They shared coffee and warm gingerbread, and bits of gossip.

"You don't think that I just stopped by for a visit, do you, Millie? Men make promises to discuss this, and figure out that; but, in truth, they don't mean it. So, it's up to us women.

"I miss you two, and I'm sure Sam does. The place is too big for just us. It feels like half the family is missing. If you prefer living here, then that's okay. I just want you to think it through carefully.

"I don't figure you should clean house or prepare meals; I can do that. I'm sure I'll need advice on how to cook to suit LC and Buc and Fred, but I do know how. Besides, they often eat in the ranch dining room. They will have to give me a chance. Sam's still alive and kicking. Will you at least give it a thought?"

"No."

"Oh." Leanna felt so let down.

"Fred and I would love to move back. We just weren't sure about your feelings. We'll never give up this piece of land. It's where we started out. We need to come here sometimes. When Sam and the boy were left alone we went down. Been there lots of years. That's as much our home as this is. We love the activity that surrounds the main ranch.

"I don't want to hear none of this hogwash about me lying around and being head of an advisory committee. We'll work out a plan that will satisfy each of us. I do fly off once in a while. But I'm sure you have your moments, too."

"We just didn't want to interfere."

"If you do interfere, I'll scream."

"Then it's a deal. Once in a while separation is good; then we'll break away and come up here for a spell."

Leanna was on her feet. They clasped each other's hands and circled around the cozy kitchen filled with spicy smells. They looked like two schoolgirls on the playground.

"It will seem more like a family again. I'll be watching out the kitchen window for you."

"By the way, I don't do windows."

"Me neither. We'll just hope it rains once in a while."

As Millie walked with Leanna to the car, Leanna's happy look faded. She confided to Millie, "Only one more problem, and that one hurts the most and has me stumped."

"Give it some room, Leanna. Some solutions take more time than others. Patience. In the meantime, let your own light shine. Don't cheat yourself, or us, out of that. Give it your best shot. This is not your sadness alone. Another party is involved. It's important for her to meet you halfway. We all want a happy outcome. Try to think of other things. Don't worry about what you don't have. Think of what you do have."

By Sunday, Millie and Fred were settled in. Monday would be a new start. Leanna was looking forward to it.

The grandfather clock in the hallway had struck ten times as Sam walked into the kitchen for a quick cup of coffee. He was leaning up against the counter. Without saying much, he wanted to convey his feelings about having Millie and Fred at the house again.

Just then footsteps came pounding across the porch. The door swung open and there stood Leanna wearing a furious look on her face.

"Samuel James Pride, what did you tell those guys?"

Sam came close to spilling coffee down his front. "I told them to teach you to jingle."

"They are treating me like a fine lady. I feel like I should be wearing a velvet dress and hat to match and be riding side saddle. Are you going to speak to them or shall I tell them what I think?"

"I'll . . . I'll talk to them again. I think you are letting this thing with Cindy get under your skin and affect everything you do. I understand about you being upset, but don't let it ruin your life."

Leanna stared at him. The sparks from her eyes could have set a barn on fire. He should never have made the remark. It was like throwing an explosive device at an already injured man. He wanted to apologize, but it was too late.

"Shut up!" With that Leanna slammed the door and pounded down the steps.

Sam turned to Millie, "Looks like the honeymoon is over. The new husband had just made a major mistake. Any ideas?"

"I'd suggest you get your tail to the corral and straighten that out; as for the rest, you're on your own."

As they drove the horses out that night, the men were on the edge of being gruff. She'd asked for it. They got right down to business.

"Get that one, Leanna, don't let him get into the bushes. Leanna, on your far right, chase her down."

The horses seemed to be unruly. Leanna suspected they were being prodded into acting up. She saw nothing that would prove this; it was just a feeling. She was working hard, and having the time of her life with the challenge.

Millie, Fred, and Sam waited supper, to see what the atmosphere would be like. Footsteps came slowly across the porch. The three were holding their breath.

The door opened with purpose. There on the threshold stood a very dusty lady with a big smile on her face and her hands on her hips. "That's more like it. I've got to shower before I eat."

Three people sighed with relief.

Sam walked up to Leanna and whispered in her ear, "Do you need any assistance?"

She gave him a whopper of a kiss and wiped the dust from her cheeks unto his. "I'll be right down."

• • •

Later that week Sam left for a two-day meeting in Midland. They had decided it would be best if he stayed over.

It was cool but the sunshine made the morning quite comfortable. Leanna put on a sweater and walked out to the road to pick up the mail. Her feeling of contentment was as welcome as the sunshine itself.

Opening the box she stared in horror. On top of the mail lay what appeared to be a rat. There was a small piece of cardboard propped against the dripping body. She had no idea who would do such a thing, nor why.

The words were scribbled but readable. "You and your daughter have stolen me and my girl's chances for a decent future. I have taken the life of the one thing you both love."

Leanna then realized that it was the body of Tinker. Feeling faint, she was holding on to the side of the box to steady herself.

LC, not knowing Leanna had gone ahead of him, was going out to get the mail. When he spotted her she was throwing up in the grasses by the box. He ran to help. "What?"

She pointed to the open mailbox. Reading the note he reached for the small limp body. Lifting it gently he placed it in the large flannel lined pocket of his jeans jacket. The little fellow was still warm. He closed his eyes momentarily. She had to have drowned the pup just minutes before.

Leanna spoke. "Why must that sweet little innocent creature have to pay for something I did?"

"You did nothing wrong. She is a sick person. I'll bury him up next to the old brown dog. They'll be good company for each other."

"I can't imagine how she did it. No one noticing her. Wouldn't Dancer have kicked up a fuss, someone taking away one of her babies?"

"I don't know, Missus. Sometimes it's better we don't know things."

"LC, for now anyway, will you tell Cindy that you found the runt dead this morning? You had said it was common, nature's way of taking care of things. She'll be sad, but accept that."

"Let me get rid of the note, or at least hide it. I'll take care of the mail so no one will know about the wet envelopes. I'm going to get you inside and tell Millie you aren't feeling well, that you went up to lie down and rest. She is like a witch, that one. There is a wild animal loose in her brain. I shall keep an eye on this woman."

• • •

Later that afternoon Jeremy swung the police car up by the back door. As Leanna came into the kitchen, she was concerned about the look of urgency on his face.

"Mrs. Taylor is dead. I'm to inform Quincy. I think she's going to need you. Will you come with me?" he pleaded. "She's at work."

"Yes, of course. Give me a minute to throw on a clean blouse and gather my wits. One thing, find LC. It's important that he know. I'll be right out. Meet you in the car."

"Looks like suicide. According to the engineer she was waiting on the road just west of town. He tooted the horn. Just before he reached the crossroad, she drove onto the track. He thought it was deliberate. No way he could stop."

"The chief sent one of the boys over to her place. There was a note on the kitchen table. Something about knowing she had done some bad things over the years, especially in recent months. Claiming this was the only way she knew to get it stopped."

Leanna ran her fingers across her forehead. She needed to be of help to Taylor. Play it by ear, she thought; help me to do the best I can.

They pulled up at the back by the overflowing garbage cans. The odor didn't help the situation any. Going inside, Jeremy quickly explained things to the restaurant owner. Quincy spied him and came back by the kitchen. It was then that Taylor saw Leanna, who was taking her old jacket she wore to work from the rack by the door.

The three of them stood by the car and Jeremy explained the circumstances. It was not a good setting for such terrible news, but it had to be done without delay.

Leanna, watching Taylor's face, saw the look of sadness. She could tell that Taylor's mind was trying to sort it all out. Before their eyes she seemed to grow older. A look of exhaustion overtook her and her knees buckled.

Jeremy lifted her into the back seat. Leanna sat next to her.

"Take us to the ranch. She's to stay with us for a few days, until things are taken care of."

Millie had overheard enough to know the basics. She figured they'd come back here. The door opened and she motioned up the stairs next to the master bedroom. Leanna stopped Jeremy from going any further.

"Millie and I will help her upstairs and stay with her. You get back to work. I know she needs you. But not right now. Come after work. You can have supper with her."

"But I . . ."

"Later."

The outpouring of love from the two women soon had Taylor bathed, in a warm nightshirt, and asleep in a short while. It was fitful sleep but eventually she rested. Leanna sat next to the bed.

The aroma of Millie's supper began wafting up the stairs. Taylor stirred and looked at Leanna. "Is it true?"

Leanna shook her head yes, and took her hand.

"I have no tears. Does that make me a bad person?"

Leanna shook her head no. They sat there in the twilight, saying nothing.

They heard the door open downstairs and Jeremy's voice.

"I love him."

"I know. I'll go down and send him up; later, I'll bring a tray up for both of you. Tomorrow you should try to get up for breakfast. I sent Jeremy by your trailer to pick up a few extra clothes. We have to take care of some things."

Two steps at a time brought Jeremy to her door, and he tapped lightly, then disappeared inside.

Leanna looked up the minister's secondary number and was glad that he answered right away. "Tuck?"

"I heard."

"I have a young lady here whom I think needs your assistance. What has happened appears to be a relief rather than a loss. Understandable as that may be, in this case, that carries guilt with it. Could you come for breakfast, just as a guest? Then you can take it from there. I'm not sure she wants to speak to you. But I'd feel better if you stopped by. We do need some help on proper arrangements."

Jeremy went home early to catch up on some sleep.

Leanna stepped in to say goodnight and to assure the girl that she was close by. Taylor looked frail. She patted the bed and asked if Leanna would sit with her.

"After my father died, my mother began to change. She seemed to think everyone was to blame for us being alone. First, it was a stiff-upper-lip attitude. We'd show 'em. We'd make it in spite of them.

"I think she'd always taken a fancy to Sam. The two couples had been friends. Maybe because the women had been school chums. He was polite but at the same time seemed to go out of his way to avoid her. As the years passed that infuriated her more and more. She became bitter about everything.

"I tried to convince her to see a doctor. That really made her mad. As I grew older she began to do some odd unexplainable things. I became afraid of her. The hate in her eyes when I moved out scared me.

"I still wanted to think of her as my mother, but gradually I tried to forget her existence. The relationship became frightening. Am I making any sense? I don't want to be crazy. I began to wonder if she was."

Leanna laughed softly. "No, my dear, there is nothing wrong with you. I am going to sit here and sing. You will either fake sleep so I will go away, or fall to sleep because of boredom."

Leanna began to sing some of the lullabies that she used to sing to Cindy when she was a baby. As much as she loved this girl, she wanted her own girl back.

When she climbed into her own bed, she wished someone would come and sing to her.

Tuck joined them for breakfast, bringing his joyful spirit along. As it worked out, he and Taylor walked the grounds. When they returned she was renewed by their discussion and refreshed by the air.

With Tuck's help all arrangements were completed. Leanna accompanied him to the driveway. "Thank you, Tuck. Your presence was appreciated." Leanna watched him drive away. She wondered if he ever questioned his choice of occupations. He was so perfect for the job.

Sam arrived home that evening. He had heard about the accident at the gas station in town. After the house was quiet, he and Leanna lay in bed and she filled him in on the details.

The funeral was the following day. Jeremy sat next to Quincy and Leanna and Sam next to him, as family. People came out of respect for Quincy Taylor, not the deceased.

Afterward, Cindy hugged Taylor and spoke with her quietly. She looked toward Leanna and nodded. Was it a beginning? Leanna glanced at Tuck and he smiled. Was it a ray of hope?

Taylor slept at the ranch that night. Monday morning she was the first one up. She and Millie prepared breakfast. She was dressed in her fresh uniform and insisted on serving everyone, just to get back in the habit.

By 7:15 she was on the road into town. "Best thing for me is to get back to work. The regulars will be glad to see me." She assured them that she would be fine.

Leanna and Millie went to the porch to wave good-bye. Millie turned to Leanna, "Well, she's got us as family, the reverend as counsel, and Jeremy to love her. I'd say things are in good shape."

"I think she will blossom and flourish. She's been carrying a heavy burden all these years. Her mother's place will have to be cleared out and there're affairs to be straightened, but I think she'll make quick order of it."

Leanna and Sam were planning to attend the big local celebration on the 25th. On the following Monday, however, a phone call came in that changed everything.

"One more meeting, Leanna, I'm sorry. Thought we were finished but we've got to iron out a couple of details."

"I've not said much about what we've been trying to accomplish. It has to do with federal land and grazing rights and some other environmental details. We need to get things worded just right so our representative can present it to Congress at the end of the month. It's extremely important to the area's future."

"After that, my dear, I'm yours. No more meetings."

Leanna didn't believe that. She had married a man who worked hard at living. Having him be different would be disappointing.

They went riding several times. Although it was enjoyable, she could tell that his mind was elsewhere.

Friday, he left. Leanna hoped that when he returned he could once again concentrate on his own land and its guests. He was proud of the environmental programs that they ran for school groups. Maybe it would build a better future for the land and its people.

She decided against attending the festivities the next day. When she went for the first time, she wanted Sam by her side.

 CHAPTER 23

It had been present in every conversation for months: save the last Saturday in October. It was the area horse show and sale, rodeo, carnival, county fair. The whole shebang rolled into one. Everyone was looking forward to it. It would begin early in the morning, ending with a dance and beer tent. If a person had any good sense he would be on his way home before the last event. That was reported, by hearsay, of course, as being wild and wooly.

Cindy and Jimmy left home at 6:00 a.m. When they arrived things were humming as if it was already mid-day. Breakfast on the grounds was served under a green and white awning. There were mounds of fried potatoes, eggs and meat, and sourdough biscuits baked over coals in heavy iron-covered pots. The smells from the open air cooking made everyone ravenous.

"Yoo-hoo, over here, here we are," could be heard above the combination of noises. Second to that was laughter. Cindy couldn't imagine who was watching the home front.

Music, dust, animals, dust; plus, the smell of roasted peanuts and fried onions. Mouths became dry from tasting the dust; that was good for the lemonade sales.

Free advice was passed out. Hold on to your money, the crowd was not all local. All the shellacking was not done at the old-fashioned shell game.

Millie's cherry pie won first prize. Wranglers were hanging around the tent, hoping to be chosen as judges.

There were some horse races after lunch. If viewers took their eyes off the racers, they could spot small groups of men exchanging bills in out-of-the-way places.

After supper, when the shadows began to extend across the grass on the infield, Cindy and Jimmy headed for the horse sale. Knowing she had never attended such an event, Jimmy insisted.

"I'll not explain anything. You turn your neck as if it was a swivel chair. Take it all in. I'll answer any of your questions tomorrow. I was brought up on this, and it's still exciting, even to me."

The outside area was full of tack and supplies, some new, some used, all for sale.

As they stepped inside, the atmosphere took a quick turnabout. Cindy experienced a closed-in feeling. A look at the faces told her this was serious business.

The men's shirts were darkened by sweat. Cigarette smoke hovered in the still air. The heavy stench of the men, their smokes, and horse manure turned Cindy's stomach upside down. A boy was constantly cleaning up after the horses, but the heat inside the building did not allow the odor to escape.

Cindy wished she'd skipped the Elephant Ears. Her stomach had been a little queasy lately. The essence of the horses at the ranch was associated with clean air and freshness.

Many of the spectators had that telltale ring on their hip pockets where they carried their Copenhagen Long Cut.

The man sitting next to her had a foam cup in his hand; she thought he was drinking coffee. Every once in a while he would bring the cup to his mouth, with his hand partially covering the top. Eventually, it dawned on her that he was spitting tobacco juice. Even the thought of sticking a plug of tobacco in her cheek or lower lip had Cindy's stomach perform another flip-flop. Imagining what it would taste like made her shudder.

She tried to hide her reaction. There were few women present. She didn't want to show her distress, nor embarrass Jimmy by needing to be escorted outside.

Minutes later, when the action started, she felt better. Concentrating on the scene being played out before her was fascinating. You could feel the vibration of people's lives.

There were different reasons for the exchange. Many ranges of emotions traveled around those corrugated walls: elation, anger, relief, disgust.

The horses were as different as the people. Some were placid, some frightened, one or two mean-acting. The ages and training differed as well. Some were shined up like the used cars in the local lot. One stood out as mistreated. He was almost as grubby-looking as his owner.

Although she understood little of what the auctioneer was doing, the sing-song of his voice was catchy. She was careful not to move for fear that she would end up the owner of a nag and be the laughing stock of the county.

Jimmy touched her elbow. "Time to head for home." The gate to the sale arena closed behind them. The coolness of the evening felt so good, Cindy took a deep breath to clean out her lungs. As they headed for the car the ruckus started.

• • •

The radio lines were open to Jeremy, his partner Buddy, the sheriff and fire department, and the cruiser on the grounds. Jeremy was part of the sheriff's posse. He knew how to respond. Having spotted the commotion, he turned his horse's head in that direction; he pressed button 4, which officially alerted the others.

A quick glance had him on the portable radio. "Officer needs assistance; loose horse, out of control. Two men down."

Buddy was beside him instantly, working back the milling crowd. Then he jumped from his mount as he saw one of the men aiming a rifle at the horse's head. Buddy forced the barrel straight up. The shot brought the chaos to a standstill. People began to move back and follow instructions.

Under his breath Buddy said to the shooter, "Put that back into your pick-up. You know better than to discharge a weapon where there are people gathered. I'll talk to you later."

Billie O could smell death before the humans around him could. He snorted with fear. The gunshot on top of the beating, the hatred, the strangers, the noises from the rides on the midway, the sirens was too much.

Billie O, with a wild look in his eyes, was ready to lunge for an escape route. Buddy calmly walked up to the horse. In a soft voice he began to talk to him. Leading him off to the side, he walked him around to calm him down.

In the meantime Jeremy instinctively knew that one of the two men on the ground was dead. He bent to his friend Jimmy, tapping on his chest. No blood from the nose. He checked vitals, all the time trying to get some response with his voice. Immediately, he called 911, which would bring the E-Unit from the barn area.

It was then that he realized Cindy was kneeling on the other side of Jimmy. She was as white as his mother's bleached sheets. Jeremy chucked her under the chin. "Hey, I'm pretty sure he's gonna be okay."

As they were loading Jimmy into the unit, Cindy caught sight of LC working his way toward them. "I'll ride in with the ambulance. Will you see if you can move the horse to the ranch? I don't think he's a maverick. I'm thinking he just needs some kindness."

"I'll take care of it. I'll also get your mom into the hospital, and we'll get hold of Sam."

Cindy's voice was a plea, "He'll be all right, won't he LC?"

"He's a lot tougher than you know, Mrs."

Cindy hopped into the front seat and the siren pierced the evening air.

• • •

As LC made his way to the police car his mind was on Cindy's lack of emotion as to what had happened. He would have expected this response from a longtime rancher's wife, but not from a beginner from out of state. He must warn Leanna to watch for the shock to wear off.

He was proud of her, thinking of Billie O, and he felt her judgment was correct. She was learning fast.

The officer and LC were old friends. "The ranch is registered and has a license with the county as an animal rescue house for the Humane Society. How would it be if I were to get the horse out of here? If you need to check him over you'd know where to find him. It might help get the crowd's mind on other things."

"As soon as they move the old man out, go ahead."

LC stood with his hands behind his back talking to the officer. "Billie O is a beautiful horse even though he's a mixed breed. He wasn't gelded 'til he was five, which can make them hard to handle. I can't recall when the old man got ahold of him.

"It was a well-known fact that he treated the horse bad. Yet never bad enough for anyone to step in and do anything. No one made a bid on him at the sale. That must be what ticked the old fella off; he hadn't even bothered to clean him up."

A drunk staggered over to the two men. "I saw the whole show, officer. It was a crowd-pleaser all right. Heh! Heh!"

The officer took a step forward. LC moved his hand up and touched his ear, looking his friend in the eye, who then paused and continued to listen to the witness.

"Billie was rearing up when the kid stepped in. He twitched the horse. It woulda worked but the old fool got mad 'cause of the interference. He used a few cuss words I ain't heard afore. Hope I can remember 'em.

"He turned and started beatin' on the kid. Threw the kid off balance and he let go. O Billie reared up. The kid fell. I'd guess a dislocated shoulder. Passed out from pain. Maybe a broken rib or two. Who knows about his innards?

"Old man turns back on the horse again. Ole Billie clamps his teeth on the old man's arm, lifts him off his feet and heaves him against the horse trailer. 'Magine he broke his neck. Horse knew it was finished. Kinda wish it hadn't been over. Like to see the horse trample him. Stuff like that gets me excited."

LC moved his head in agreement with the story.

The policeman with authority and speed twisted the drunk's arm behind his back and clamped the cuffs on him. Opening the cruiser's rear door, he jostled him inside.

"You don't have to manhandle me," the drunk whined.

The officer willfully ignored him.

LC caught sight of one of the ranch hands and instructed him to wait to see that Billie O got to the stables okay. He needed to pick up Leanna and get her to the hospital to be with Cindy.

• • •

The staff was waiting at the emergency entrance and rushed Jimmy into a separate room. Cindy was steered toward the waiting room and informed that they could do a better job with her out of the way.

The room was empty. She didn't know if this was to her liking. Should she scream or throw herself against the wall? She had never been this scared. What do you do when your insides felt like they are going to explode? She wanted to be calm and strong and helpful, but she was too afraid.

No nurse came with good news or bad. The quiet was far worse than the noise of the celebration where they had spent the day. She could only think of one word, which she uttered repeatedly. "Please." Looking out the window she realized how dark it was outside and wondered what time it was. It didn't matter. What difference did the time make? How long had they been here? Why didn't someone tell her something?

When Leanna, Gramps, and LC entered the room she was sitting with her eyes closed, rocking back and forth. Leanna touched her on the shoulder. "Cindy." Cindy's eyes flew open and she jerked back from her mother's touch and looked away.

Leanna put her hand to her mouth and backed up. Cindy needed someone she could trust. Leanna walked to the window, struggling to hold back tears. She stared down at the lights in the parking lot but they became blurred. She knew that losing control would help no one. Remaining at the window, out of Cindy's vision, seemed to be the only answer. Why did a daughter, who had always loved her, shut her out?

Cindy turned toward her mother with a hateful look in her eyes. "You don't know how I feel, do you? You seem to always win and never lose. If Jimmy dies, then I've lost everything. Where will my life go then?"

The white plastic chair she was sitting in began to shake violently and she sobbed uncontrollably. No one moved.

Leanna looked like she was going to fall to the floor, her face crumbling like a shattered mirror.

• • •

Jimmy came to, just enough to wonder where he was. Then he heard the swishing sound of the nurse's uniform and smelled the disinfectant.

There was so much pain throughout his body that the sounds and smells were welcome. He didn't recollect why he was here, but he accepted it as a godsend. As his memory began to fade again he could think of only one thing. "Cin, I'm sorry. I love you. I'll be okay." Then he slipped into oblivion.

• • •

LC quietly slipped out of the waiting room. This was private and it was wrong for him to be here. Driving back to the ranch he was confident that he could help Billie O with his war. The truck was pulling in just ahead of him. He followed the dirt-covered tail-lights of the old horse trailer to the barn. The two unhooked the trailer. LC then turned to the ranch hand. "If you want to go back to the dance, that's fine. I'll tend to the horse from here on in." The man grinned and hopped back in the truck. "Still a lot of night left."

LC waited until the night silence returned. He walked to the barn and began preparing a stall.

* * *

Around midnight a call came into the station. A timid voice inquired, "Have you arrested Joe Smith again?"

"Yes, Ma'am, he's in the drunk tank." After a moment's silence he heard a sigh of relief.

"Thank you, officer."

• • •

When LC got near the trailer again he switched to his native tongue. A bit rusty, but the horse wouldn't know. It had been a long time. As he spoke, he slowly moved Billie O into the yard and walked him inside. He cleaned the blood away and put salve on the welts. His voice remained a monotone as he gently massaged the horse's body. Moving to the next stall he rearranged some straw, and the two of them slept.

• • •

When Cindy quieted a little, she realized she was looking at Gramps's pant legs and old worn-out work shoes. Raising her eyes to his face, she was overwhelmed at what she saw in his eyes. There was a look of sadness and regret.

"Stand up, and listen up, young lady. You are not a young lady, but a grown woman; it's time you got yourself straightened around. You are thinking of yourself and no one else. Your mother deserves love."

Cindy blurted out, "But from someone else, not Sam."

"So, that's the crux of the thing. Just as I suspected. Why not Sam? They love one another very much and you are deeply hurting them both with this attitude."

"It just seems wrong."

Gramps's tone became gentler. "Can you tell me why?"

"I'm not sure."

"Are you jealous?"

Cindy looked horrified.

"Had he become a father figure?"

Cindy hung her head and murmured, "Yes."

"That was extremely important to you. It filled a terrible void. You felt that part of him belonged to you. Did you think that if he loved anyone else they would be taking him from you? At the same time you felt guilty. You are cheating him of a full life, and in this case, also you are cheating your own mother.

"Suppose he had married someone else. How would you have felt then?"

Cindy looked confused. "I'm not sure."

"You've got to remember, your mother didn't just fall for him, he fell in love with her. They deserve the kind of love they can give each other. Their hearts still have plenty of room to love you, too. We make a great family but we've got to stick together, not fight among ourselves."

Cindy put her head in her hands. "What have I done? I didn't realize. Oh, Gramps, will they forgive me?"

Leanna was listening to all of this in a daze.

The door was pushed open and Sam entered the room with his long strides. He saw Cindy's swollen eyes and tear-stained face and thought the worst, but he went directly to Leanna and wrapped his arms around her. "I came as soon as they reached me." Then his arms included Cindy, also encompassing Gramps.

Gramps looked at Cindy. "You see how big his arms are? His heart is like that, too. There is enough love for us all."

Sam began to relax a little; although Cindy had been crying extensively, this did not appear to be a death watch.

Just then the doctor came through the door and walked toward them. "Everything has been checked. Jimmy will be fine, in time. He'll take some mending, and knowing him, he'll be impatient and get ornery."

"Broken collar bone, a couple of ribs, concussion from when he hit the wagon. According to the officer, the horse reared up. I'd say Jimmy tried to hold on to control him, so he hit the ground hard. Plus the old man's beating; he is going to be sore, sore, and beyond. We don't find any signs of internal damage. We are keeping him a few days just to make sure there's no surprises. We'll sedate him enough to relieve the pain. I do imagine he'll be a bear when he gets home, for a while. Not much we can do, it will just take time."

Cindy kissed her mom on the cheek; she stood back and said, "I can't tell you how sorry I am." Then moving close she hugged her mom, resting her head on her chest like she did as a small child. Cindy then turned to Sam. "Forgive me for not loving you enough." Turning to Gramps she winked and said, "Thank you. Will you always watch over me, as my protective angel?"

Gramps moved over toward the coffee machine, and reaching in his overall pocket he retrieved his blue hankie. He was dabbing at his eyes when a yellow waitress uniform came flying through the door. Taylor was gasping for breath.

She could tell by the smiling faces that the world had not stopped. "Jeremy came and picked me up as soon as he could. He's in the elevator. I took the stairs."

Sam looked at Leanna and Gramps. "Has there been something else going on here?"

They smiled at each other. "Just a little family discussion."

The doctor turned to Cindy. "Jimmy will need your strength and understanding. There is something strange that I should mention. He keeps mumbling. It sounds like he's saying sin, and how sorry he is."

That got a laugh from Cindy. "That's Cin, with a capital C. He's telling me he's sorry and he loves me. Since my feelings are the same, and I need his strength also, could I see him now?"

Cindy put her shoulders back and her chin up and put her arm through the doctor's arm. Before the door closed behind them, those gathered in the waiting room heard Cindy's clear strong voice echo back down the hallway. "By the way, Doc, don't you worry. This family can handle anything. Working together, nothing or nobody can beat us."

About the Author

As a young girl Donna Bocks wrote poetry emulating her beloved Auntie. While in college her oral storytelling was popular with roommates—"tell us a story" was the constant request. When her children arrived, Donna loved to rock them in the rocking chair and sing original story-songs spun from their everyday lives. Her literary impulses were piqued by an author interview. Afterward she realized that she could actually write down the stories in her head.

Most of Donna's novels are set in Michigan where she was born 78 years ago. "Stories happen," says Donna, "walking everyday in the neighborhood. The houses begin to speak and the stories grow street by street, house by house." Donna's oldest son asked her to take him on a walk and point out the elements of one of her novels. He was delighted as street names became names of characters, and as his familiar surroundings were sprinkled with his mother's magic storytelling dust!

The author welcomes correspondence from her readers:
P. O. Box 8231, Holland, Michigan 49422-8231
DonnaBocks@birthAbook.com

About the Illustrator

Tom Ball has always loved to draw. He studied art and architectural drawing throughout high school. To relieve the intensity of his chosen profession in law enforcement, he draws. When the family goes camping, he sketches, and his daughter does too. Tom is a two-time Olympian, having served on security details at both the Atlanta and Salt Lake City Olympics. He is the husband of Colleen, father of Travis and Sarah, and proud walker of Aspen, an English Springer Spaniel.